Astounding S

April ,1931

Various

Alpha Editions

This edition published in 2024

ISBN : 9789367243367

Design and Setting By
Alpha Editions
www.alphaedis.com
Email - info@alphaedis.com

MONSTERS OF MARS

A COMPLETE NOVELETTE

By Edmond Hamilton

The Martian gestured with a reptilian arm toward the ladder.

Allan Randall stared at the man before him. "And that's why you sent for me, Milton?" he finally asked.

There was a moment's silence, in which Randall's eyes moved as though uncomprehendingly from the face of Milton to those of the two men beside him. The four sat together at the end of a roughly furnished and electric-lit living-room, and in that momentary silence there came in to them from the outside night the distant pounding of the Atlantic upon the beach. It was Randall who first spoke again.

> Three Martian-duped Earth-men swing open the gates of space that for so long had barred the greedy hordes of the Red Planet.

The other's face was unsmiling. "That's why I sent for you, Allan," he said quietly. "To go to Mars with us to-night!"

"To Mars!" he repeated. "Have you gone crazy, Milton—or is this some joke you've put up with Lanier and Nelson here?"

Milton shook his head gravely. "It is not a joke, Allan. Lanier and I are actually going to flash out over the gulf to the planet Mars to-night. Nelson must stay here, and since we wanted three to go I wired you as the most likely of my friends to make the venture."

"But good God!" Randall exploded, rising. "You, Milton, as a physicist ought to know better. Space-ships and projectiles and all that are but fictionists' dreams."

"We are not going in either space-ship or projectile," said Milton calmly. And then as he saw his friend's bewilderment he rose and led the way to a door at the room's end, the other three following him into the room beyond.

It was a long laboratory of unusual size in which Randall found himself, one in which every variety of physical and electrical apparatus seemed represented. Three huge dynamo-motor arrangements took up the room's far end, and from them a tangle of wiring led through square black condensers and transformers to a battery of great tubes. Most remarkable, though, was the object at the room's center.

It was like a great double cube of dull metal, being in effect two metal cubes each twelve feet square, supported a few feet above the floor by insulated standards. One side of each cube was open, exposing the hollow interiors of the two cubical chambers. Other wiring led from the big electronic tubes and from the dynamos to the sides of the two cubes.

The four men gazed at the enigmatic thing for a time in silence. Milton's strong, capable face showed only in its steady eyes what feelings were his, but Lanier's younger countenance was alight with excitement; and so too to some degree was that of Nelson. Randall simply stared at the thing, until Milton nodded toward it.

"That," he said, "is what will flash us out to Mars to-night."

Randall could only turn his stare upon the other, and Lanier chuckled. "Can't take it in yet, Randall? Well, neither could I when the idea was first sprung on us."

Milton nodded to seats behind them, and as the half-dazed Randall sank into one the physicist faced him earnestly.

"Randall, there isn't much time now, but I am going to tell you what I have been doing in the last two years on this God-forsaken Maine coast. I have been for those two years in unbroken communication by radio with beings on the planet Mars!

"It was when I still held my physics professorship back at the university that I got first onto the track of the thing. I was studying the variation of static vibrations, and in so doing caught steady signals—not static—at an unprecedentedly high wave-length. They were dots and dashes of varying length in an entirely unintelligible code, the same arrangement of them being sent out apparently every few hours.

"I began to study them and soon ascertained that they could be sent out by no station on earth. The signals seemed to be growing louder each day, and it suddenly occurred to me that Mars was approaching opposition with earth! I was startled, and kept careful watch. On the day that Mars was closest the earth the signals were loudest. Thereafter, as the red planet receded, they grew weaker. The signals were from some being or beings on Mars!

"At first I was going to give the news to the world, but saw in time that I could not. There was not sufficient proof, and a premature statement would only wreck my own scientific reputation. So I decided to study the signals farther until I had irrefutable proof, and to answer them if possible. I came up here and had this place built, and the aerial towers and other equipment I wanted set up. Lanier and Nelson came with me from the university, and we began our work.

"Our chief object was to answer those signals, but it proved heartbreaking work at first. We could not produce a radio wave of great enough length to pierce out through earth's insulating layer and across the gulf to Mars. We used all the power of our great windmill-dynamo hook-ups, but for long could not make it. Every few hours like clockwork the Martian signals came through. Then at last we heard them repeating one of our own signals. We had been heard!

"For a time we hardly left our instruments. We began the slow and almost impossible work of establishing intelligent communication with the Martians. It was with numbers we began. Earth is the third planet from the sun and Mars the fourth, so three represented earth and four stood for Mars. Slowly we felt our way to an exchange of ideas, and within months were in steady and intelligent communication with them.

"They asked us first concerning earth, its climates and seas and continents, and concerning ourselves, our races and mechanisms and weapons. Much information we flashed out to them, the language of our communication being English, the elements, of which they had learned, with a mixture of numbers and symbolical dot-dash signals.

"We were as eager to learn about them. They were somewhat reticent, we found, concerning their planet and themselves. They admitted that their world was a dying one and that their great canals were to make life possible on it, and also admitted that they were different in bodily form from ourselves.

"They told us finally that communication like this was too ineffective to give us a clear picture of their world, or vice versa. If we could visit Mars, and then they visit earth, both worlds would benefit by the knowledge of the other. It seemed impossible to me, though I was eager enough for it. But the Martians said that while spaceships and the like were impossible, there was a way by which living beings could flash from earth to Mars and back by radio waves, even as our signals flashed!"

Randall broke in in amazement. "By radio!" he exclaimed, and Milton nodded.

"Yes, so they said, nor did the idea of sending matter by radio seem too insane, after all. We send sound, music by radio waves across half the world from our broadcasting stations. We send light, pictures, across the world from our television stations. We do that by changing the wave length of the light-vibrations to make them radio vibrations, flashing them out thus over the world, to receivers which alter their wave-lengths again and change them back into light-vibrations.

"Why then could not matter be sent in the same way? Matter, it has been long believed, is but another vibration of the ether, like light and radiant heat and radio vibrations and the like, having a lower wave-length than any of the others. Suppose we take matter and by applying electrical force to it change its wave-length, step it up to the wave-length of radio vibrations? Then those vibrations can be flashed forth from the sending station to a special receiver that will step them down again from radio vibrations to matter vibrations. Thus matter, living or non-living, could be flashed tremendous distances in a second!

"This the Martians told us, and said they would set up a matter-transmitter and receiver on Mars and would aid and instruct us so that we could set up a similar transmitter and receiver here. Then part of us could be flashed out to Mars as radio vibrations by the transmitter, and in moments would have flashed across the gulf to the red planet and would be transformed back from radio vibrations to matter-vibrations by the receiver awaiting us there!

"Naturally we agreed enthusiastically to build such a matter-transmitter and receiver, and then, with their instructions signalled to us constantly, started the work. Weeks it took, but at last, only yesterday, we finished it. The thing's two cubical chambers are one for the transmitting of matter and the other for its reception. At a time agreed on yesterday we tested the thing, placing a guinea pig in the transmitting chamber and turning on the actuating force. Instantly the animal vanished, and in moments came a signal from the

Martians saying that they had received it unharmed in their receiving chamber.

"Then we tested it the other way, they sending the same guinea pig to us, and in moments it flashed into being in our receiving chamber. Of course the step-down force in the receiving chamber had to be in operation, since had it not been at that moment the radio-vibrations of the animal would have simply flashed on endlessly in endless space. And the same would happen to any of us were we flashed forth and no receiving chamber turned on to receive us.

"We signalled the Martians that all tests were satisfactory, and told them that on the next night at exactly midnight by our time we would flash out ourselves on our first visit to them. They have promised to have their receiving chamber operating to receive us at that moment, of course, and it is my plan to stay there twenty-four hours, gathering ample proofs of our visit, and then flash back to earth.

"Nelson must stay here, not only to flash us forth to-night, but above all to have the receiving chamber operating to receive us at the destined moment twenty-four hours later. The force required to operate it is too great to use for more than a few minutes at a time, so it is necessary above all that that force be turned on and the receiving chamber ready for us at the moment we flash back. And since Nelson must stay, and Lanier and I wanted another, we wired you, Randall, in the hope that you would want to go with us on this venture. And do you?"

As Milton's question hung, Randall drew a long breath. His eyes were on the two great cubical chambers, and his brain seemed whirling at what he had heard. Then he was on his feet with the others.

"Go? Could you keep me from going? Why, man, it's the greatest adventure in history!"

Milton grasped his hand, as did Lanier, and then the physicist shot a glance at the square clock on the wall. "Well, there's little enough time left us," he said, "for we've hardly an hour before midnight, and at midnight we must be in that transmitting chamber for Nelson to send us flashing out!"

Randall could never recall but dimly afterward how that tense hour passed. It was an hour in which Milton and Nelson went with anxious faces and low-voiced comments from one to another of the pieces of apparatus in the room, inspecting each carefully, from the great dynamos to the transmitting and receiving chambers, while Lanier quickly got out and made ready the rough khaki suits and equipment they were to take.

It lacked but a quarter-hour of midnight when they had finally donned those suits, each making sure that he was in possession of the small personal kit Milton had designated. This included for each a heavy automatic, a small supply of concentrated foods, and a small case of drugs chosen to counteract the rarer atmosphere and lesser gravity which Milton had been warned to expect on the red planet. Each had also a strong wrist-watch, the three synchronized exactly with the big laboratory clock.

When they had finished checking up on this equipment the clock's longer hand pointed almost to the figure twelve, and the physicist gestured expressively toward the transmitting chamber. Lanier, though, strode for a moment to one of the laboratory's doors and flung it open. As Randall gazed out with him they could see far out over the tossing sea, dimly lit by the great canopy of the summer stars overhead. Right at the zenith among those stars shone brightest a crimson spark.

"Mars," said Lanier, his voice a half-whisper. "And they're waiting out there for us now—out there where we'll be in minutes!"

"And if they shouldn't be waiting—their receiving chamber not ready—"

But Milton's calm voice came across the room to them: "Zero hour," he said, stepping up into the big transmitting chamber.

Lanier and Randall slowly followed, and despite himself a slight shudder shook the latter's body as he stepped into the mechanism that in moments would send him flashing out through the great void as impalpable ether-vibrations. Milton and Lanier were standing silent beside him, their eyes on Nelson, who stood watchfully now at the big switchboard beside the chambers, his own gaze on the clock. They saw him touch a stud, and another, and the hum of the great dynamos at the room's end grew loud as the swarming of angry bees.

The clock's longer hand was crawling over the last space to cover the smaller hand. Nelson turned a knob and the battery of great glass tubes broke into brilliant white light, a crackling coming from them. Randall saw the clock's pointer clicking over the last divisions, and as he saw Nelson grip a great switch there came over him a wild impulse to bolt from the transmitting chamber. But then as his thoughts whirled maelstromlike there came a clang from the clock and Nelson flung down the switch in his grasp. Blinding light seemed to break from all the chamber onto the three; Randall felt himself hurled into nothingness by forces titanic, inconceivable, and then knew no more.

Randall came back to consciousness with a humming sound in his ears and with a sharp pain piercing his lungs at every breath. He felt himself lying on a smooth hard surface, and heard the humming stop and be succeeded by a complete silence. He opened his eyes, drawing himself to his feet as Milton and Lanier were doing, and stared about him.

He was standing with his two friends inside a cubical metal chamber almost exactly the same as the one they had occupied in Milton's laboratory a few moments before. But it was not the same, as their first astounded glance out through its open side told them.

For it was not the laboratory that lay around them, but a vast conelike hall that seemed to Randall's dazed eyes of dimensions illimitable. Its dull-gleaming metal walls slanted up for a thousand feet over their heads, and through a round aperture at the tip far above and through great doors in the walls came a thin sunlight. At the center of the great hall's circular floor stood the two cubical chambers in one of which the three were, while around the chambers were grouped masses of unfamiliar-looking apparatus.

To Randall's untrained eyes it seemed electrical apparatus of very strange design, but neither he nor Milton nor Lanier paid it but small attention in that first breathless moment. They were gazing in fascinated horror at the scores of creatures who stood silent amid the apparatus and at its switches, gazing back at them. Those creatures were erect and roughly man-like in shape, but they were not human men. They were—the thought blasted to Randall's brain in that horror-filled moment—crocodile-men.

Crocodile-men! It was only so that he could think of them in that moment. For they were terribly like great crocodile shapes that had learned in some way to carry themselves erect upon their hinder limbs. The bodies were not covered with skin, but with green bony plates. The limbs, thick and taloned at their paw-ends, seemed greater in size and stronger, the upper two great arms and the lower two the legs upon which each walked, while there was but the suggestion of a tail. But the flat head set on the neckless body was most crocodilian of all, with great fanged, hinged jaws projecting forward, and with dark unwinking eyes set back in bony sockets.

Each of the creatures wore on his torso a gleaming garment like a coat of metal scales, with metal belts in which some had shining tubes. They were standing in groups here and there about the mechanisms, the nearest group at a strange big switch-panel not a half-dozen feet from the three men. Milton and Lanier and Randall returned in a tense silence the unwinking stare of the monstrous beings around them.

"The Martians!" Lanier's horror-filled exclamation was echoed in the next instant by Randall's.

"The Martians! God, Milton! They're not like anything we know—they're reptilian!"

Milton's hand clutched his shoulder. "Steady, Randall," he muttered. "They're terrible enough, God knows—but remember we must seem just as grotesque to them."

The sound of their voices seemed to break the great hall's spell of silence, and they saw the crocodilian Martians before them turning and speaking swiftly to each other in low hissing speech-sounds that were quite unintelligible to the three. Then from the small group nearest them one came forward, until he stood just outside the chamber in which they were.

Randall felt dimly the momentousness of the moment, in which beings of earth and Mars were confronting each other for the first time in the solar system's history. The creature before them opened his great jaws and uttered slowly a succession of sounds that for the moment puzzled them, so different were they from the hissing speech of the others, though with the same sibilance of tone. Again the thing repeated the sounds, and this time Milton uttered an exclamation.

"He's speaking to us!" he cried. "Trying to speak the English that I taught them in our communication! I caught a word—listen...."

As the creature repeated the sounds, Randall and Lanier started to hear also vaguely expressed in that hissing voice familiar words: "You—are Milton and—others from—earth?"

Milton spoke very clearly and slowly to the creature: "We are those from earth," he said. "And you are the Martians with whom we have communicated?"

"We are those Martians," said the other's hissing voice slowly. "These"—he waved a taloned paw toward those behind him—"have charge of the matter-transmitter and receiver. I am of our ruler's council."

"Ruler?" Milton repeated. "A ruler of all Mars?"

"Of all Mars," the other said. "Our name for him would mean in your words the Martian Master. I am to take you to him."

Milton turned to the other two with face alight with excitement. "These Martians have some supreme ruler they call the Martian Master," he said quickly; "and we're to go before him. As the first visitors from earth we're of immense importance here."

As he spoke, the Martian official before them had uttered a hissing call, and in answer to it a long shape of shining metal raced into the vast hall and halted beside them. It was like a fifty-foot centipede of metal, its scores of supporting short legs actuated by some mechanism inside the cylindrical body. There was a transparent-walled control room at the front end of that body, and in it a Martian at the controls who snapped open a door from which a metal ladder automatically descended.

The Martian official gestured with a reptilian arm toward the ladder, and Milton and Lanier and Randall moved carefully out of the cube-chamber and across the floor to it, each of their steps being made a short leap forward by the lesser gravity of the smaller planet. They climbed up into the centipede-machine's control room, their guide following, and then as the door snapped shut, the operator of the thing pulled and turned the knob in his grasp and the long machine scuttled forward with amazing smoothness and speed.

In a moment it was out of the building and into the feeble sunlight of a broad metal-paved street. About them lay a Martian city, seen by their eager eyes for the first time. It was a city whose structures were giant metal cones like that from which they had just come, though none seemed as large as that titanic one. Throngs of the hideous crocodilian Martians were moving busily to and fro in the streets, while among them there scuttled and flashed numbers of the centipede-machines.

As their strange vehicle raced along, Randall saw that the conelike structures were for the most part divided into many levels, and that inside some could be glimpsed ranks of great mechanisms and hurrying Martians tending them. Away to their right across the vast forest of cones that was the city the sun's little disk was shining, and he glimpsed in that direction higher ground covered with a vast tangle of bright crimson jungle that sloped upward from a great, half-glimpsed waterway.

The Martian beside them saw the direction of his gaze and leaned toward him. "No Martians live there," he hissed slowly. "Martians live only in cities where canals meet."

"Then there's no life in those crimson jungles?" Randall asked, repeating the question a moment later more slowly.

"No Martians there, but life—living things," the other told him, searching for words. "But not intelligent, like Martians and you."

He turned to gaze ahead, then pointed. "The Martian Master's cone," he hissed.

The three saw that at the end of the broad metal street down which their vehicle was racing there loomed another titanic cone-structure, fully as large as the mighty one in which they first found themselves. As the centipede-machine swept up to its great door-opening and halted, they descended to the metal paving and then followed their reptilian guide through the opening.

They found themselves in a great hall in which scores of the Martians were coming and going. At the hall's end stood a row of what seemed guards, Martians grasping shining tubes such as they had already glimpsed. These gave way to allow their passage when their conductor uttered a hissing order, and then they were moving down a shorter hall at whose end also were guards. As these sprang aside before them, a great door of massive metal they guarded moved softly upward, disclosing a mighty circular hall or room inside. Their crocodilian guide turned to them.

"The hall of the Martian Master," he hissed.

They passed inside with him. The great hall seemed to extend upward to the giant cone's tip, thin light coming down from an opening there. Upon the dull metal of its looming walls were running friezes of lighter metal, grotesque representations of reptilian shapes that they could but vaguely glimpse. Around the walls stood rank after rank of guards.

At the hall's center was a low dias, and in a semicircle around and behind it stood a half-hundred great crocodilian shapes. Randall guessed even at the moment that they were the council of which their conductor had named himself a member. But like Milton and Lanier, he had eyes in that first moment only for the dais itself. For on it was—the Martian Master.

Randall heard Milton and Lanier choke with the horror that shook his own heart and brain as he gazed. It was not simply another great crocodilian shape that sat upon that dais. It was a monstrous thing formed by the joining of three of the great reptilian bodies! Three distinct crocodile-like bodies sitting close together upon a metal seat, that had but a single great head. A great, grotesque crocodilian head that bulged backward and to either side, and that rested on the three thick short necks that rose from the triple body! And that head, that triple-bodied thing, was living, its unwinking eyes gazing at the three men!

The Martian Master! Randall felt his brain reel as he gazed at that mind-shattering thing. The Martian Master—this great head with three bodies!

Reason told Randall, even as he strove for sanity, that the thing was but logical, that even on earth biologists had formed multiple-headed creatures by surgery, and that the Martians had done so to combine in one great head, one great brain, the brains of three bodies. Reason told him that the great triple brain inside that bulging head needed the bloodstreams of all three bodies to nourish it, must be a giant intellect indeed, one fitted to be the supreme Martian Master. But reason could not overcome the horror that choked him as he gazed at the awful thing.

A hissing voice sounding before him made him aware that the Martian Master was speaking.

"You are the Earth-beings with whom we communicated, and whom we instructed to build a matter-transmitter and receiver on earth?" the slow voice asked. "You have come safely to Mars by means of that station?"

"We have come safely." Milton's voice was shaken and he could find no other words.

"That is well. Long had we desired to have such a station built on earth, since with it there to flash back and forth between the two worlds is easy. You have come, then, to learn of this world and to take back what you learn to your races?"

"That is why we came." Milton said, more steadily. "We want to stay only hours on this first visit, and then flash back to earth as we came."

The head's awful eyes seemed to consider them. "But when do you intend to go back?" its strange voice asked. "Unless the one at your earth station has its receiver operating at the right moment you will simply flash on endlessly as radio waves—will be annihilated."

Milton found the courage to smile. "We started from earth at our midnight exactly, and at midnight exactly twenty-four earth hours later, we are to flash back and the receiver will be awaiting us."

There was silence when he had said that, a silence that seemed to Randall's strained mind to have become suddenly tense, sinister. The great triple-bodied creature before them considered them again, its eyes moving over them, and when it again spoke the hissing words came very slowly.

"Twenty-four earth hours," it said; "and then your receiver on earth will be awaiting you. That time we can measure to the moment, and that is well. For it is not you three Earth-beings who will flash back to earth when that moment comes! It will be Martians, the first of our Martian masses who have waited for ages for that moment and who will begin then our conquest of the earth!

"Yes, Earth-beings, our great plan comes to its end now at last! At last! Age on age, prisoned on this dying, arid world, we have desired the earth that by right of power shall be ours, have sought for ages to communicate with its beings. You finally heard us, you hearkened to us, you built the matter-transmitting and receiving station on earth that was the one thing needed for our plan. For when the matter-receiver of that station is turned on in twenty-four of your hours, and ready to receive matter flashes from here, it will be the first of our millions who will flash at last to earth!

"I, the Martian Master, say it. Those first to go shall seize that matter-receiver on earth when first they appear there, shall build other and larger receivers, and through them within days all our Martian hordes shall have been flashed to earth! Shall have poured out over it and conquered with our weapons your weak races of Earth-beings, who cannot stand before us, and whose world you have delivered at last into our hands!"

For a moment, when the great monster's hissing voice had ceased, Milton and Randall and Lanier gazed toward it as though petrified, the whole unearthly scene spinning about them. And then, through the thick silence, the thin sound of Milton's voice:

"Our world—our earth—delivered to the Martians, and by us! God—no!"

With that last cry of agonized comprehension and horror, Milton did what surely had never any in the great hall expected, leaped onto the dais with a single spring toward the Martian Master! Randall heard a hundred wild hissing cries break from about him, saw the crocodilian forms of guards and council rushing forward even as he and Lanier sprang after Milton, and then glimpsed shining tubes levelled from which brilliant shafts of dazzling crimson light or force were stabbing toward them!

To Randall the moment that followed was but a split-second flash and whirl of action. As his earthly muscles took him forward with Lanier after Milton in a great leap to the dais, he was aware of the brilliant red rays stabbing behind him closely, and knew that only the tremendous size of his leap had taken him past them. In the succeeding instant he was made aware of what he had escaped, for the hastily-loosed rays struck squarely a group of three or four Martian guards rushing to the dais from the opposite side, and they vanished from view with a sharp detonation as though clicked out of existence!

Randall was not to know then, that the red rays were ones that annihilated matter by neutralizing or damping the matter-vibrations in the ether. But he did know that no more rays were loosed, for by then he and Milton and Lanier were on the dais and were wrapped in a hurricane combat with the guards that had rushed between them and the Martian Master.

Gleaming fangs—great scaled forms—reaching talons—it was all a wild phantasmagoria of grotesque forms spinning around him as he struck with all the power of his earthly muscles and felt crocodilian forms staggering and going down beneath his frenzied blows. He heard the roar of an automatic close beside him in the melee as Milton remembered at last through the red haze of his fury the weapon he carried, but before either Randall or Lanier could reach their own weapons a new wave of crocodilian forms had poured onto them that by sheer pressing weight held them helpless, to be disarmed.

Hissing orders sounded, the arms and legs of the three were tightly grasped by great taloned paws, and the masses of Martians about them melted back from the dais. Held each by two great creatures, Milton and Randall and Lanier faced again the triple-bodied Martian Master, who in all that wild moment of struggle appeared not to have changed his position. The big monster's black eyes stared unmovedly down at them.

"You Earth-beings seem of lower intelligence even than we thought," his hissing voice informed them. "And those weapons—crude, very crude."

Milton, his face set, spoke back: "It may be that you will find human weapons of some power if your hordes reach earth," he said.

"But what compared with the power of ours?" the other asked coldly. "And since our scientists even now devise new weapons to annihilate the earth's races, I think they would be glad of three of those races to experiment with now. The one use we can make of you, certainly."

The creature turned its bulging head a little towards the guards who held the three men, and uttered a brief hissing order. Instantly the six Martians, grasping the three tightly, marched them across the great hall and through a different door than that by which they had entered.

They were taken down a narrow corridor that turned sharply twice as they went on. Randall saw that it was lit by squares inset in the walls that glowed with crimson light. It came to him as they marched on that night must be upon the Martian city without, since the sun had been sinking when they had crossed it in the centipede-machine.

Through what seemed an ante-room they were taken, and then into a long hall instantly recognizable as a laboratory. There were many glowing squares illuminating it, and narrow windows high in the wall gave them a glimpse of the city outside, a pattern of crimson lights. Long metal tables and racks filled the big room's farther end, while along the walls were ranged shining mechanisms of unfamiliar and grotesque appearance. Fully a score of the crocodilian Martians were busy in the room, some intent on their work at the racks and tables, others operating some of the strange machines.

The guards conducted the three to an open space by the wall, below one of the high window-openings and between two great cylindrical mechanisms. Then, while five of their number held the three men prisoned in that space by the threat of their levelled ray-tubes, the other moved toward one of the busy Martian scientists and held with him a brief interchange of hissing speech.

Milton leaned to whisper to the other two: "We've got to get out of this while we're still living," he whispered. "You heard the Martian Master—in constructing that matter-receiver on earth, we've opened a door through which all the Martian millions will pour onto our world!"

"It's useless, Milton," said Randall dully. "Even if we got clear of this the Martians will be at their matter-transmitter in hordes when the moment comes to flash back to earth."

"I know that, but we've got to try," the other insisted. "If we or some of us could get clear of this, we might in some way hide near the matter-transmitter until the moment came and then fight to it."

"But how to get out of the hands of these, even?" asked Lanier, nodding toward the alert guards before them.

"There's but one way," Milton whispered swiftly. "Our earthly muscles would enable us, I think, to get through this window-opening above us in a leap, if we had a moment's chance. Well, whichever of us they take to experiment with or examine first, must make a struggle or disturbance that will turn the guards' attention for a moment and give the other two a chance to make the attempt!"

"One to stay and the other two to get away...." Randall said slowly; but Milton's tense whisper interrupted:

"It's the only way, and even then a thousand to one chance! But it's we who have opened this gate for the Martian invasion of our world and it's we who must—"

Before he could finish, the approach of hissing voices told them that the leader of the six guards and the Martian who seemed the chief of the experimenters in the hall were nearing them. The three men stood silent and tense as the two crocodilian monsters stopped before them. The scientist, who carried in his metal-belt, instead of a ray-tube a compact case of instruments, surveyed them as though in curiosity.

He came closer, his quick reptilian eyes taking in with evident interest every feature of their bodily appearance. Intuitively the three knew that one of them was to be chosen for a first investigation by the Martian scientists, and that that one would have not even the slender hope of escape open to the other two. A strange lottery of life and death!

Randall saw the creature's gaze turn from one to another of them, and then heard the hiss of his voice as he pointed a taloned paw toward Milton. Instantly two of the guards had seized Milton and had jerked him out from the wall, the other guards holding back Randall and Lanier with threatening tubes. It was upon Milton that the fatal choice had fallen!

Randall and Lanier made together a half-movement forward, but Milton, a tense message in his eyes, forced them back. The guards who held the physicist led him, at the direction of the Martian scientist, toward a great upright frame at the room's far end, upon which were clustered a score of dial-indicators. From these flexible cords led; and now the scientists began attaching these by clips to various spots on Milton's body. Some mechanical examination of his bodily characteristics were apparently to be made. Milton shot suddenly a glance at the two by the wall, and his head nodded in an almost imperceptible signal. The muscles of Lanier and Randall tensed.

Then abruptly Milton seemed to go mad. He shouted aloud in a terrible voice, and at the same moment tore from him the cords just attached, his fists striking out then at the amazed Martians around him. As they leaped back from that sudden explosion of activity and sound on Milton's part the guards before Randall and Lanier whirled instinctively for an instant toward it. And in that instant the two had leaped.

It was upward they leaped, with all the force of their earthly muscles, toward the big window-opening a half-dozen feet in the wall above them. Like released steel springs they sat up, and Randall heard the thump of their feet as they struck the opening's sill, heard wild cries suddenly coming from beneath them, as the guards turned back toward them. Crimson rays clove up like light toward them, but the instant's surprise had been enough, and in it they had leaped on and through the opening, into the outside night!

As they shot downward and struck the metal paving outside, Randall heard a wild babble of cries from inside. A moment he and Lanier gazed frenziedly around them, then were running with great leaps along the base of the building from which they had just escaped.

In the darkness of night the Martian city stretched away to their right, its massive dark cone-structures outlined by points of glowing ruddy light here and there upon them. Beside the city's metal streets were illuminated by the brilliant field of stars overhead and by the soft light of the two moons, one much larger than the other, that moved among those stars.

Along the street crocodilian Martians were coming and going still, though in small numbers, there being but few in sight in the dim-lit street's length. Lanier pointed ahead as they leaped onward.

"Straight onward, Randall!" he jerked. "There seem fewer of the Martians this way!"

"But the great cone of the matter-station is the other way!" Randall exclaimed.

"We can't risk making for it now!" cried the other. "We've got to keep clear of them until the alarm is over. Hear them now?"

For even as they leaped forward a rising clamor of hissing cries and rush of feet was coming from behind as scores of Martians poured out into the darkness from the great cone-building. The two fugitives had passed by then from the shadow of the mighty structure, and as they ran along the broad metal street toward the shadow of the next cone, through the light of the moons above, they heard higher cries and then glimpsed narrow shafts of crimson force cleaving the night around them.

Randall, as the deadly rays drove past him, heard the low detonating sound made by their destruction of the air in their path, and the inrush of new air. But in the misty and uncertain moonlight the rays could not be loosed accurately, and before they could be swept sidewise to annihilate the two fleeing men they had gained, with a last great leap, the shadow of the next building.

On they ran, the clatter of the Martian pursuit growing more noisy behind them. Randall heard Lanier gasping with each great leap, and felt himself at every breath a knife of pain stabbing through his lungs, the rarified atmosphere of the red planet taking its toll. Again from the darkness behind them the crimson rays clove, but this time were wide of their mark.

With every moment the clamor of pursuit seemed growing louder, the alarm spreading out over the Martian city and arousing it. As they raced past cone after cone, Randall knew even the increased power of their muscles could not long aid them against the exhaustion which the thin air was imposing on them. His thoughts spun for a moment to Milton, in the laboratory behind, and then back to their own desperate plight.

Abruptly shapes loomed in the misty light before them! A group of three great Martians, reptilian shapes that had been coming toward them and had stopped for an instant in amazement at sight of the running pair. There was no time to halt themselves, to evade the three, and with a mutual instinct Lanier and Randall seized together the last expedient open to them. They ran straight forward toward the astounded three, and when a half-score feet from them, leaped with all their force upward and toward them, their tensed bodies flying through the air with feet outstretched before them.

Then they had struck the group of three with feet-foremost, and with the impetus of that great leap had knocked them sprawling to this side and that, while with a supreme effort the two kept their balance and leaped on. The cries of the three added to the din behind them as they threw themselves forward.

They flung themselves past a last cone building to halt for an instant in utter amazement despite the nearing pursuit. Before them were no more streets and structures, but a huge smooth-flowing waterway! It gleamed in the moonlight and lay at right angles across their path, seeming to flow along the Martian city's edge.

"A canal!" cried Lanier. "It's one of the canals that meet at this city and flow around it! We're trapped—we've reached the city's edge!"

"Not yet!" Randall gasped. "Look!"

As he pointed to the left Lanier shot a glance there; and then both of them were running in that direction, along the smooth metal paving that bordered the mighty canal. They came to what Randall had seen, a mighty metal arch that soared out over the waterway to its opposite side. A bridge!

They were on it, were racing up the smooth incline of it. Randall glanced back as they reached the arch's summit. From that height the city stretched far away behind them, a lace of crimson lights in the night. He glimpsed the gleam of the giant waterway that encircled the city completely, one that was fed by other canals from far away that emptied into it, the great city's vital water-supply brought thus from this world's melting polar snows.

There were moving lights behind now, too, pouring out onto the metal paving by the waterway, moving to and fro as though in confusion, with a babel of hissing cries. It was not until Randall and Lanier were running down the descending incline of the great arched bridge, though, that the lights and shouts of their pursuers began to move up on that bridge after them.

Running off the bridge's smooth way, the two found themselves stumbling on through the darkness over more metal paving, and then over soft ground. There were no lights or buildings or sounds of any sort on this farther side of the great waterway. A tall dark wall seemed suddenly to loom up out of the darkness some distance ahead of the two.

"The crimson jungle!" Randall cried. "The jungles we glimpsed from the city! It's a chance to hide!"

They raced toward the protecting blackness of that wall of vegetation. They reached it, flung themselves inside, just as the pursuing Martians, a mass of running crocodilian shapes and of great racing centipede-machines, swept up over the bridge's arch behind. A moment the two halted in the thick vegetation's shelter, gasping for breath, then were moving forward through the jungle's denser darkness.

Thick about them and far above them towered the masses of strange trees and plant life through which they made their way. Randall could see but dimly the nature of these plant-forms, but could make out that they were grotesque and unearthly in appearance, all leafless, and with masses of thin tendrils branching from them instead of leaves. He realized that it was only beside the arid planet's great canals that this profusion of plant life had sufficient moisture for existence, and that it was the broad bands of jungle bordering the canals that had made the latter visible to earth's astronomers.

Lanier and he halted for a moment to listen. The thick jungle about them seemed quite silent. But from behind there came through it a vague tumult of hissing calls; and then, as they glimpsed red flashes far behind, they heard the crashing of great masses of the leafless trees.

"The rays!" whispered Lanier. "They're beating through the jungle with them and the centipede-machines after us!"

They paused no more, but pushed on through the thick growths with renewed urgency. Now and then, as they passed through small clearings, Randall glimpsed overhead the fast-moving nearer moon and slower sailing farther moon of Mars, moving across the steady stars. In some of these clearings they saw, too, strange great openings burrowed in the ground as though by some strange animal.

The crashing clamor of the Martians beating the jungle behind was coming close, ever closer, and as they came to still another misty-lit clearing, Lanier paused, with face white and tense.

"They're closing in on us!" he said. "They're hunting us down by beating the jungle with those centipede-machines, and even if we escape them we're getting farther from the city and the matter-station each moment!"

Randall's eyes roved desperately around the clearing; and then, as they fell on a group of the great burrowed openings that seemed present everywhere about them, he uttered an exclamation.

"These holes! We can hide in one until they've passed over us, and then steal back to the city!"

Lanier's eyes lit. "It's a chance!"

They sprang toward the openings. They were each of some four feet diameter, extending indefinitely downward as though the mouths of tunnels. In a moment Randall was lowering himself into one, Lanier after him. The tunnel in which they were, they found, curved to one side a few feet below the surface. They crawled down this curve until they were out of sight of the opening above. They crouched silent, then, listening.

There came down to them the dull, distant clamor of the centipede-machines crashing through the jungle, cutting a way with rays, their clamor growing ever louder. Then Randall, who was lowest in the tunnel, turned suddenly as there came to him a strange rustling sound from *beneath* him. It was as though some crawling or creeping thing was moving in the tunnel below them!

He grasped the arm of Lanier, beside and a little above him, to warn him, but the words he was about to whisper never were uttered. For at this moment a big shapeless living thing seemed to flash up toward them through the darkness from beneath, cold ropelike tentacles gripped both tightly; and then in an instant they were being dragged irresistibly down into the lightless tunnel's depths!

As they were pulled swiftly downward into the tunnel by the tentacles that grasped them an involuntary cry of horror came from Randall and Lanier alike. They twisted frantically in the cold grip that held them, but found it of the quality of steel. And as Randall twisted in it to strike frantically down through the darkness at whatever thing of horror held them, his clenched fist met but the cold smooth skin of some big, soft-bodied creature!

Down—down—remorselessly they were being drawn farther into the black depths of the tunnel by the great thing crawling down below them. Again and again the two twisted and struck, but could not shake its hold. In sheer exhaustion they ceased to struggle, dragged helplessly farther down.

Was it minutes or hours, Randall wondered afterward, of that horrible progress downward, that passed before they glimpsed light beneath? A feeble glow, hardly discernible, it was, and as they went lower still he saw that it was caused by the tunnel passing through a strata of radio-active rock that gave off the faint light. In that light they glimpsed for the first time the horror dragging them downward.

It was a huge worm creature! A thing like a giant angleworm, three feet or more in thickness and thrice that in length, its great body soft and cold and worm-like. From the end nearest them projected two long tentacles with which it had gripped the two men and was dragging them down the tunnel after it! Randall glimpsed a mouth-aperture in the tentacled end of the worm body also, and two scarlike marks above it, placed like eyes, although eyes the monstrous thing had not.

But a moment they glimpsed it and then were in darkness again as the tunnel passed through the radio-active strata and lower. The horror of that moment's glimpse, though, made them strike out in blind repulsion, but relentlessly the creature dragged them after it.

"God!" It was Lanier's panting cry as they were dragged on. "This worm monster—we're hundreds of feet below the surface!"

Randall sought to reply, but his voice choked. The air about them was close and damp, with an overpowering earthy smell. He felt consciousness leaving him.

A gleam of soft light—they were passing more radio-active patches. He felt the wild convulsive struggles of Lanier against the thing; and then suddenly the tunnel ended, debouched into a far-stretching, low-ceilinged cavity. It was feebly illuminated by radio-active patches here and there in walls and ceiling, and as the monster that held them halted on entering the cavity, Randall and Lanier lay in its grip and stared across the weird place with intensified horror.

For it was swarming with countless worm monsters! All were like the one who held them, thick long worm bodies with projecting tentacles and with black eyeless faces. They were crawling to and fro in this cavern far beneath the surface, swarming in hordes around and over each other, pouring in and out of the awful place from countless tunnels that led upward and downward from it!

A world of worm monsters, beneath the surface of the Martian jungles! As Randall stared across that swarming, dim-lit cave of horror, physically sick at sight of it, he remembered the countless tunnel openings they had glimpsed in their flight through the jungle, and remembered the remark of the Martian who had first guided them across the city, that in the jungles were living things, of a sort. These were the things, worm monsters whose unthinkable networks of tunnels and burrows formed beneath the surface a veritable worm world!

"Randall!" It was Lanier's thick exclamation. "Randall—those scar-marks on their—faces—you see—?"

"See?"

"Those marks! These creatures had eyes once but must have been forced down here by the Martians. These may once have been—ages ago—human!"

At that thought Randall felt horror overcoming his senses. He was aware that the great worm monster holding them was dragging them forward through the cavern, that others of the swarms there were crowding around them, feeling them blindly with their tentacles, helping to drag them forward.

Half-carried and half-dragged they went, scores of tentacles now holding them, great worm shapes crawling forward on all sides of them and accompanying them along the cavern's length. He glimpsed worm monsters here and there emerging from the upward tunnels with masses of strange plant stuff in their grasp that others blindly devoured. His senses reeled from the suffocating air, the great cavity being but a half-score feet in height, burrowed from the damp earth by these numberless things.

The faint, strange light of the radio-active patches showed him that they were approaching the cavern's end. Tunnels opened from its end as from all its walls and floor, and into one Randall was dragged by the creatures, one before and one behind, grasping him, and Lanier being brought behind him in the same way. In the close tunnel the heavy air was deadly, and he was but partly conscious when again, after moments of crawling along it, he felt himself dragged out into another cavern.

This earth-walled cavity, though, seemed to extend farther than the first, though of the same height as the first and with a few radio-active illuminating patches. In it seethed and swarmed literally hundreds on hundreds of the worm monsters, a sea of great crawling bodies. Randall and Lanier saw that they were being carried and dragged now toward the farther end of this larger cavity.

As they approached it, pushing through the swarming creatures who felt them with inquisitive tentacles as their captors took them forward, the two men saw that a great shape was looming up in the faint light at the cave's far end. In moments they were close enough to discern its nature, and a horror and awe filled them at sight of it more intense than they had yet felt.

For the looming shape was a huge earthen image or statue of a worm! It was shaped with a childish crudeness from the solid earth, a giant earthen worm shape whose body looped across the cave's end, and whose tentacled head or front end was reared upward to the cavity's roof. Before this awful earthen shape was a section of the cave's floor higher than the rest, and on it a great crudely shaped rectangular earthen block.

"Lanier—that shape!" whispered Randall in his horror. "That earthen image, made by these creatures—it's the worm god they've made for themselves!"

"A worm god!" Lanier repeated, staring toward it as they were dragged nearer. "Then that block...."

"Its altar!" Randall exclaimed. "These things have some dim spark of intelligence or memory! They're brought us here to—"

Before he could finish, the clutching tentacles of the worm monsters about them had dragged them up onto the raised floor beside the block, beneath the looming earthen worm shape. There they glimpsed for the first time in the faint light another who stood there held tightly by the tentacles of two worm monsters. It was a Martian!

The big crocodilian shape was apparently a prisoner like themselves, captured and brought down from above. His reptilian eyes surveyed Lanier and Randall quickly as they were dragged up and held beside him, but he took no other interest. To the two men, at the moment, it seemed that his great crocodilian shape was human, almost, so much more man-like was it than the grotesque worm monsters before them.

With a half-dozen of the creatures holding the two men and the Martian tightly, another great worm monster crawled to the edge of the raised earth floor in front of the giant worm god's image, and then reared up the first third of his thick body into the air. By then the great, faint-lit cavity stretching before them was filled with countless numbers of the monsters, pouring into it from all the tunnels that opened into it from above and below, packing it thick with their grotesque bodies as far as the eye could reach in the dim light.

They were seething and crawling in that great mass; but as the worm monster on the elevation upreared, all in the cavity seemed suddenly to quiet. Then the upreared eyeless thing began to move his long tentacles. Very slowly at first he waved them back and forth, and slowly the masses of monsters in the cavity, all turned by some sense toward him, did likewise, the cavity becoming a forest of upraised tentacles waving rhythmically back and forth in unison with those of the leader.

Back and forth—back and forth—Randall felt caught in some torturing nightmare as he watched the countless tentacle-feelers waving thus from one side to the other. It was a ceremony, he knew—some strange rite springing perhaps from dim memory alone, that these worm monsters carried out thus before the looming shape of their worm god. Only the six that held the three captives never relaxed their grip.

Still on and on went the strange and senseless rite. By then the close, damp air of that cavity far beneath Mars' surface was sinking Randall and Lanier deeper into a half-consciousness. The Martian beside them never moved or spoke. The upstretched tentacles of the leader and of the great worm horde before him never ceased swaying rhythmically from side to side.

Randall, half-hypnotized by those swaying tentacles and but semi-conscious by then, could only estimate afterward how long that grotesque rite went on. Hours it must have endured, he knew, hours in which each opening of his eyes revealed only the dimly-illuminated cavern, the worm monsters that filled it, the forest of tentacles waving in unison. It was only toward the end of those hours that he noticed vaguely that the tentacles were waving faster and faster.

And as the tentacles of leader and worm horde waved alike ever more swiftly an atmosphere of growing excitement and expectation seemed to hold the horde. At last the upstretched feelers were whipping back and forth almost too swiftly for the eye to follow. Then abruptly the worm leader ceased the motion himself, and while the horde before him continued it, turned and crawled to the three captives.

I In an instant, as though in answer to a second command, the two worm monsters who held the Martian dragged him forward toward the great earthen block before the worm god's image. Two others of the creatures came from the side, and the four swiftly stretched the Martian flat on the block's top, each of the four grasping with their tentacles one of his four taloned limbs. They seemed to hesitate then, the worm leader beside them, the tentacles of the horde waving swiftly still.

Abruptly the tentacles of the leader flashed up as though in a signal. There was a dull ripping sound, and in that moment Randall and Lanier saw the Martian on the block torn literally limb from limb by the four great worm monsters who had held his four limbs!

The tentacles of the horde waved suddenly with increased, excited swiftness at that. Randall shrank in horror.

"They've brought us here for that!" he cried. "To sacrifice us on that altar that way to their worm god!"

But Lanier too had cried out, appalled, as he saw that awful sacrifice, and both strained madly against the grip of the worm creatures. Their struggles were in vain, and then in answer to another unspoken command the two monsters that held Randall were dragging him also to the earthen altar!

He felt himself gripped by the four great creatures around the block, felt as he struggled with his last strength that he was being stretched out on the block, each of the four at one of its corners grasping one of his limbs. He heard Lanier's mad cries as though from a great distance, glimpsed as he was held thus on his back the great shape of the earthen worm god reared over him, and then glimpsed the leader of the monsters rearing beside him.

The dull sound of the swift-waving tentacles of the horde came to him, there was a tense moment of agony of waiting, and then the tentacles of the leader flashed up in the signal!

But at the same moment Randall felt his limbs released by the four monsters that had held them! There seemed sudden wild confusion in the great cave. The strange rite broke off; the horde of worm monsters crawled frantically this way and that in it. Randall slipped off the block; staggered to his feet.

The worm monsters in the cave were swarming toward the downward tunnel openings! The two captives forgotten, the creatures were pouring in crawling, fighting swarms toward those openings. And then, as Randall and Lanier stared stupefied, there came a red flash from one of the upward tunnels and a brilliant crimson ray stabbed down and mowed a path of annihilation in the cave's earthen side!

The two heard great thumping sounds from above, saw the tunnels leading from above becoming suddenly many times greater in size as red rays flashed down along them to gouge the tunnel's walls. Then down from those enlarged tunnels there were bursting long shining shapes, great centipede-machines crawling down the tunnels which their rays made larger before them! And as the centipede-machines burst down into the cavern their crimson rays stabbed right and left to cut paths of annihilation among the worms.

"The Martians!" Lanier cried. "They didn't find us above—they knew we must have been taken by these things—and they've come down after us!"

"Back, Lanier!" Randall shouted. "Quick, before they see us, behind this—"

As he spoke he was jerking Lanier with him behind the looming earthen statue of the great worm god. Crouched there between the statue and the cave's wall they were hidden precariously from the view of those in the cavern. And now that cavern had become a scene of horror unthinkable as the centipede-machines pouring down into it blasted the frantically crawling worm monsters with their rays.

The worm monsters attempted no resistance, but sought only to escape into their downward tunnels, and in moments those not caught by the rays had vanished in the openings. But the centipede-machines, after racing swiftly around the cavity, were following them, were going down into those downward tunnels also, their rays blasting down ahead of each to make the tunnel large enough for them to follow.

In a moment all but one had vanished down into the openings, the remaining one having its front or head jammed in one of the openings from the failure of its operator to blast a large enough opening before him. As Lanier and Randall watched tensely they saw the machine's control room door open and a Martian descend. He inspected the tunnel opening in which his vehicle was jammed, then with a hand ray-tube began to disintegrate the earth around that opening to free his machine.

Randall clutched his companion's arm. "That machine!" he whispered. "If we could capture it, it would give us a chance to get back to the city—to Milton and the matter-transmitter!"

Lanier started, then nodded swiftly. "We'll chance it," he whispered. "For our twenty-four hours here must be almost up."

They hesitated a moment, then crept forward from behind the great earthen statue. The Martian had his back to them, his attention on the freeing of his mechanism. Across the dim-lit cavern they crept softly, and were within a dozen feet of the Martian when some sound made him wheel quickly to confront them with the deadly tube. But even as he whirled the two had leaped.

The force of their leap sent them flying through that dozen feet of space to strike the Martian at the moment his tube levelled. One hissing call he uttered as they struck him, and then with all his strength Lanier had grasped the crocodilian body and bent it backward. Something in it snapped, and the Martian collapsed limply. The two looked wildly around.

Nothing showed that the Martian's call had been heard, and after a moment's glance that showed the head of the centipede machine already freed, they were clambering up into its control room, closing the door. Randall seized the knob with which he had seen the machines operated. As he pulled it toward him the machine moved across the tunnel opening and raced smoothly over the cavern's floor. As he turned the knob the machine turned swiftly in the same direction.

He headed the long mechanism toward one of the upward-curving tunnels which the Martians had blasted larger in descending. They were almost to it when there flashed up into the cavity from one of the downward tunnel openings a centipede-machine, and then another, and another. The Martians in their transparent-windowed control rooms took in at a glance the dead crocodilian on the floor, and then the three great machines were darting toward that of Randall and Lanier.

"The Martian we killed!" Randall cried. "They heard his call and are coming after us!"

"Turn to the wall!" Lanier shouted to him. "I have the rays—"

At that moment there was a clicking beside Randall and he glimpsed Lanier pulling forth two small grips he had found, then saw that two crimson rays were stabbing from tubes in their machine's front toward the others even as their own rays darted back. The beams that had been loosed toward them grazed past them as Randall whirled their machine to the wall, and he saw one of the three attacking mechanisms vanish as Lanier's beams struck it.

Around—back—with instinctive, lightninglike motions he whirled their centipede-machine in the great dim-lit cave as the two remaining ones leapt again to the attack. Their rays shot right and left to catch the two men's vehicle in a trap of death, and as Randall swung their own mechanism straight ahead he glimpsed at the cavern's far end the great earthen worm god still upreared.

On either side of them the red beams burned as they leapt forward, but as though running a gauntlet of death Randall kept the machine racing forward in the succeeding second until the two others loomed on either side of it. Then Lanier's beams were driving in turn to right and left of them and the two vanished as though by magic as they were struck.

"Up to the surface!" Lanier cried, his eyes on the glowing dial of his wrist-watch. "We've been held hours here—we've but a half-hour or more before earth midnight!"

Randall sent their machine racing again toward one of the upward tunnels, and as the long mechanism began to climb smoothly up the darkness he heard Lanier agonizing beside him.

"God, if we have only enough time to get to that matter-transmitter before the Martians start flashing to earth through it!"

"But Milton?" Randall cried. "We don't know whether he's alive or dead! We can't leave him!"

"We must!" said Lanier solemnly. "Our duty's to the earth now, man, to the world that we alone can save from the Martian invasion and conquest! At the hour of twelve Nelson will have the matter-receiver turned on and at that hour the Martian will start flashing to earth—unless we prevent!"

Suddenly Randall grasped the knob in his hands more tightly as light showed above them. They had been climbing upward through the enlarged tunnel at their machine's highest speed, and now as the tunnel curved the light grew stronger. Suddenly they were emerging into the thin sunlight of the Martian day.

In the crimson jungle about them were many Martians, milling excitedly to and fro, and other centipede-machines that were blasting their way down through tunnels to the worm world beneath.

Randall and Lanier, breathless, crouched low in the transparent-windowed control room as they sent their mechanism racing through this scene of swarming activity. Both gasped as one of the centipede-machines clashed against their own in passing, its Martian driver turning to stare after them. But there came no alarm, and in a moment they had passed out of the swarm of Martians and machines and were heading through the jungle in the direction of the city.

Through the weird red vegetation their mechanism raced with them, Randall holding it at its highest speed, and in minutes they came out of the jungle and were racing over the clear space between it and the great canal. Beyond that canal loomed into the thin sunlight the clustering cones of the mighty

Martian city, two towering above all the others—the cone of the Martian Master and the other cone in which was the matter-transmitter and receiver.

It was toward the latter that Lanier pointed. "Head straight toward that cone, Randall—we've but minutes left!"

They were racing now up over the great arch of the canal's metal bridge, and then scuttling smoothly off it and along the broad metal street through which they had fled in darkness hours before. In it Martians and centipede-machines were coming and going in great numbers, but none noticed the human forms of the two crouched low in their mechanism's control room.

They were rushing then toward the looming cone of the Martian Master. As they flashed past it Randall saw Lanier's face working, knew the desire that tore at him even as at himself to burst inside and ascertain whether or not Milton still lived in the laboratories from which they had fled. But they were past it, faces white and grim, were rushing on through the Martian city at reckless speed toward the other mighty cone.

It seemed that all in the great city were heading toward the same goal, streams of crocodilian Martians and masses of shining centipede-machines filling the streets as they moved toward it. As they came closer to the mighty structure, hearts pounding, they saw that around it surged a mighty mass of Martians and machines. The hordes waiting to be released through the matter-transmitter inside upon the unsuspecting earth!

"Try to get the machine inside!" Lanier whispered tensely. "If we can smash that transmitter yet...."

Randall nodded grimly. "Keep ready at the ray-tubes," he told the other.

As unobtrusively as possible he sent their long mechanism worming forward through the vast throng of machines and Martians, toward the great cone's door. Crouching low, the hands of their watches closing fast toward the twelfth figure, they edged forward in the long machine. At last they were moving through the mighty door, into the cone's interior.

They moved slowly on through the mass of machines and crocodile forms inside, then halted. For at the great crowd's center was a clear circle hundreds of feet across, and as Randall gazed across it his heart seemed to leap once and then stop.

At the center of that clear circle rose the two cubical metal chambers of the matter-transmitter and receiver. The transmitting chamber, they saw, was flooded with humming force, with white light pouring from its inner walls. It was already in operation, and the masses of Martians in the great cone were only waiting for the moment to sound when the receiver on earth would be operating also. Then they would pour into the chamber to be flashed in masses across the gulf to earth! The eyes of all in the cone seemed turned toward an erect dial-mechanism beside the chambers which was clocklike in appearance, and that would mark the moment when the first Martian could enter the transmitting-chamber and flash out.

A little distance from the two metal chambers stood a low dais on which there sat the hideous triple-bodied form of the Martian Master. Around him were the massed members of his council, waiting like him for the start of their age-planned invasion of earth. And beside the dais was a figure between two crocodilian guards at sight of whom Randall forgot all else.

"Milton! My God, Lanier, it's Milton!"

"Milton! They've brought him here to torture or kill him if they find he's lied about the moment they could flash to earth!"

Milton! And at sight of him something snapped in Randall's brain.

With a single motion of the knob he sent their centipede-machine crashing out into the clear circle at the mighty cone's center. A wild uproar of hissing cries broke from all the thousands in it as he sent the mechanism whirling toward the dais of the Martian Master. He saw the crocodilian forms there scattering blindly before him, and then as his rays drove out and spun and stabbed in mad figures of crimson death through the astounded Martian masses he saw Milton looking up toward them, crying out crazily to them as his two guards loosed him for the moment.

A high call from the Martian Master ripped across the hall and was answered by a shattering roar of hissing voices as Martians and machines surged madly toward them. Randall and Lanier in a single leap were out of the centipede-machine, and in an instant had half-dragged Milton with them in a great leap up to the edge of the humming transmitting chamber.

Milton was shouting hoarsely to them over the wild uproar. To enter that transmitting chamber before the destined moment was annihilation, to be flashed out with no receiver on earth awaiting them. They turned, struck with all their strength at the first Martians rushing up to them. No rays flashed, for a ray loosed would destroy the chamber behind them that was the one gate for the Martians to the world they would invade. But as the Martian Master's high call hissed again all the countless crocodilian forms in the great cone were rushing toward them.

Braced at the very edge of the humming, light-filled chamber, Randall and Lanier and Milton struck madly at the Martians surging up toward them. Randall seemed in a dream. A score of taloned paws clutched him from beneath; scaled forms collapsed under his insane blows.

The whole vast cone and surging reptilian hordes seemed spinning at increasing speed around him. As his clenched fists flashed with waning strength he glimpsed crocodilian forms swarming up on either side of them, glimpsed Lanier down, talons reaching toward him, Milton fighting over him like a madman. Another moment would see it ended—reptilian arms reaching in scores to drag him down—Milton jerking Lanier half to his feet. The Martian Master's call sounded—and then came a great clanging sound at which the Martian hordes seemed to freeze for an instant motionless, at which Milton's voice reached him in a supreme cry.

"Randall—the transmitter!"

For in that instant Milton was leaping back with Lanier, and as Randall with his last strength threw himself backward with them into the humming transmitting-chamber's brilliant light, he heard a last frenzied roar of hissing cries from the Martian hordes about them. Then as the brilliant light and force from the chamber's walls smote them, Randall felt himself hurled into blackness inconceivable, that smashed like a descending curtain across his brain.

The curtain of blackness lifted for a moment. He was lying with Milton and Lanier in another chamber whose force beat upon them. He saw a yellow-lit room instead of the great cone—saw the tense, anxious face of Nelson at the switch beside them. He strove to move, made to Nelson a gesture with his arm that seemed to drain all strength and life from him; and then, as in answer to it Nelson drove up the switch and turned off the force of the matter-receiver in which they lay, the black curtain descended on Randall's brain once more.

Two hours later it was when Milton and Randall and Lanier and Nelson turned to the laboratory's door. They paused to glance behind them. Of the great matter-transmitter and receiver, of the apparatus that had crowded the laboratory, there remained now but wreckage.

For that had been their first thought, their first task, when the astounded Nelson had brought the three back to consciousness and had heard their amazing tale. They had wrecked so completely the matter-station and its actuating apparatus that none could ever have guessed what a mechanism of wonder the laboratory a short time before had held.

The cubical chambers had been smashed beyond all recognition, the dynamos were masses of split metal and fused wiring, the batteries of tubes were shattered, the condensers and transformers and wiring demolished. And it had only been when the last written plans and blue-prints of the mechanism had been burned that Milton and Randall and Lanier had stopped to allow their exhausted bodies a moment of rest.

Now as they paused at the laboratory's door, Lanier reached and swung it open. Together, silent, they gazed out.

It all seemed to Randall exactly as upon the night before. The shadowy masses in the darkness, the heaving, dim-lit sea stretching far away before them, the curtain of summer stars stretched across the heavens. And, sinking westward amid those stars, the red spark of Mars toward which as though toward a magnet all their eyes had turned.

Milton was speaking. "Up there it has shone for centuries—ages—a crimson spot of light. And up there the Martians have been watching, watching— until at last we opened to them the gate."

Randall's hand was on his shoulder. "But we closed that gate, too, in the end."

Milton nodded slowly. "We—or the fate that rules our worlds. But the gate is closed, and God grant, shall never again be opened by any on this world."

"God grant it," the other echoed.

And they were all gazing still toward the thing. Gazing up toward the crimson spot of light that burned there among the stars, toward the planet that shone red, menacing, terrible, but whose menace and whose terror had been thrust back even as they had crouched to spring at last upon the earth.

Presently there was not one Robot, but three!

THE EXILE OF TIME

BEGINNING A FOUR-PART NOVEL

By Ray Cummings

CHAPTER I

Mysterious Girl

From somewhere out of Time come a swarm of Robots who inflict on New York the awful vengeance of the diabolical cripple Tugh.

The extraordinary incidents began about 1 A.M. in the night of June 8-9, 1935. I was walking through Patton Place, in New York City, with my friend Larry Gregory. My name is George Rankin. My business—and Larry's—are details quite unimportant to this narrative. We had been friends in college. Both of us were working in New York; and with all our relatives in the middle west we were sharing an apartment on this Patton Place—a short crooked, little-known street of not particularly impressive residential buildings lying near the section known as Greenwich Village, where towering office buildings of the business districts encroach close upon it.

This night at 1 A. M. it was deserted. A taxi stood at a corner; its chauffeur had left it there, and evidently gone to a nearby lunch room. The street lights were, as always, inadequate. The night was sultry and dark, with a leaden sky and a breathless humidity that presaged a thunder storm. The houses were mostly unlighted at this hour. There was an occasional apartment house among them, but mostly they were low, ramshackle affairs of brick and stone.

We were still three blocks from our apartment when without warning the incidents began which were to plunge us and all the city into disaster. We were upon the threshold of a mystery weird and strange, but we did not know it. Mysterious portals were swinging to engulf us. And all unknowing, we walked into them.

Larry was saying, "Wish we would get a storm to clear this air—*what the devil?* George, did you hear that?"

We stood listening. There had sounded a choking, muffled scream. We were midway in the block. There was not a pedestrian in sight, nor any vehicle save the abandoned taxi at the corner.

"A woman," he said. "Did it come from this house?"

We were standing before a three-story brick residence. All its windows were dark. There was a front stoop of several steps, and a basement entryway. The windows were all closed, and the place had the look of being unoccupied.

"Not in there, Larry," I answered. "It's closed for the summer—" But I got no further; we heard it again. And this time it sounded, not like a scream, but like a woman's voice calling to attract our attention.

"George! Look there!" Larry cried.

The glow from a street light illumined the basement entryway, and behind one of the dark windows a girl's face was pressed against the pane.

Larry stood gripping me, then drew me forward and down the steps of the entryway. There was a girl in the front basement room. Darkness was behind her, but we could see her white frightened face close to the glass. She tapped on the pane, and in the silence we heard her muffled voice:

"Let me out! Oh, let me get out!"

The basement door had a locked iron gate. I rattled it. "No way of getting in," I said, then stopped short with surprise. "What the devil—"

I joined Larry by the window. The girl was only a few inches from us. She had a pale, frightened face; wide, terrified eyes. Even with that first glimpse, I was transfixed by her beauty. And startled; there was something weird about her. A low-necked, white satin dress disclosed her snowy shoulders; her head was surmounted by a pile of snow-white hair, with dangling white curls framing her pale ethereal beauty. She called again.

"What's the matter with you?" Larry demanded. "Are you alone in there? What is it?"

She backed from the window; we could see her only as a white blob in the darkness of the basement room.

I called, "Can you hear us? What is it?"

Then she screamed again. A low scream; but there was infinite terror in it. And again she was at the window.

"You will not hurt me? Let me—oh please let me come out!" Her fists pounded the casement.

What I would have done I don't know. I recall wondering if the policeman would be at our corner down the block; he very seldom was there. I heard Larry saying:

"What the hell!—I'll get her out. George, get me that brick.... Now, get back, girl—I'm going to smash the window."

But the girl kept her face pressed against the pane. I had never seen such terrified eyes. Terrified at something behind her in the house; and equally frightened at us.

I call to her: "Come to the door. Can't you come to the door and open it?" I pointed to the basement gate. "Open it! Can you hear me?"

"Yes—I can hear you, and you speak my language. But you—you will not hurt me? Where am I? This—this was my house a moment ago. I was living here."

Demented! It flashed to me. An insane girl, locked in this empty house. I gripped Larry; said to him: "Take it easy; there's something queer about this. We can't smash windows. Let's—"

"You open the door," he called to the girl.

"I cannot."

"Why? Is it locked on the inside?"

"I don't know. Because—oh, hurry! If he—if it comes again—!"

We could see her turn to look behind her.

Larry demanded, "Are you alone in there?"

"Yes—now. But, oh! a moment ago he was here!"

"Then come to the door."

"I cannot. I don't know where it is. This is so strange and dark a place. And yet it was my home, just a little time ago."

Demented! And it seemed to me that her accent was very queer. A foreigner, perhaps.

She went suddenly into frantic fear. Her fists beat the window glass almost hard enough to shatter it.

"We'd better get her out," I agreed. "Smash it, Larry."

"Yes." He waved at the girl. "Get back. I'll break the glass. Get away so you won't get hurt."

The girl receded into the dimness.

"Watch your hand," I cautioned. Larry took off his coat and wrapped his hand and the brick in it. I gazed behind us. The street was still empty. The slight commotion we had made had attracted no attention.

The girl cried out again as Larry smashed the pane. "Easy," I called to her. "Take it easy. We won't hurt you."

The splintering glass fell inward, and Larry pounded around the casement until it was all clear. The rectangular opening was fairly large. We could see a dim basement room of dilapidated furniture: a door opening into a back room; the girl; nearby, a white shape watching us.

There seemed no one else. "Come on," I said. "You can get out here."

But she backed away. I was half in the window so I swung my legs over the sill. Larry came after me, and together we advanced on the girl, who shrank before us.

Then suddenly she ran to meet us, and I had the sudden feeling that she was not insane. Her fear of us was overshadowed by her terror at something else in this dark, deserted house. The terror communicated itself to Larry and me. Something eery, here.

"Come on," Larry muttered. "Let's get her out of here."

I had indeed no desire to investigate anything further. The girl let us help her through the window. I stood in the entryway holding her arms. Her dress was of billowing white satin with a single red rose at the breast; her snowy arms and shoulders were bare; white hair was piled high on her small head. Her face, still terrified, showed parted red lips; a little round black beauty patch adorned one of her powdered cheeks. The thought flashed to me that this was a girl in a fancy dress costume. This was a white wig she was wearing!

I stood with the girl in the entryway, at a loss what to do. I held her soft warm arms; the perfume of her enveloped me.

"What do you want us to do with you?" I demanded softly. McGuire, the policeman on the block, might at any moment pass. "We might get arrested! What's the matter with you? Can't you explain? Are you hurt?"

She was staring as though I were a ghost, or some strange animal. "Oh, take me away from this place! I will talk—though I do not know what to say—"

Demented or sane, I had no desire to have her fall into the clutches of the police. Nor could we very well take her to our apartment. But there was my friend Dr. Alten, alienist, who lived within a mile of here.

"We'll take her to Alten's," I said to Larry, "and find out what this means. She isn't crazy."

A sudden wild emotion swept me, then. Whatever this mystery, more than anything in the world I did not want the girl to be insane!

Larry said, "There was a taxi down the street."

It came, now, slowly along the deserted block. The chauffeur had perhaps heard us, and was cruising past to see if we were possible fares. He halted at the curb. The girl had quieted; but when she saw the taxi her face registered wildest terror, and she shrank against me.

"No! No! Don't let it kill me!"

Larry and I were pulling her forward. "What the devil's the matter with you?" Larry demanded again.

She was suddenly wildly fighting with us. "No! That—that mechanism—"

"Get her in it!" Larry panted. "We'll have the neighborhood on us!"

It seemed the only thing to do. We flung her, scrambling and fighting, into the taxi. To the half-frightened, reluctant driver, Larry said vigorously:

"It's all right; we're just taking her to a doctor. Hurry and get us away from here. There's good money in it for you!"

The promise—and the reassurance of the physician's address—convinced the chauffeur. We whirled off toward Washington Square.

Within the swaying taxi I sat holding the trembling girl. She was sobbing now, but quieting.

"There," I murmured. "We won't hurt you; we're just taking you to a doctor. You can explain to him. He's very intelligent."

"Yes," she said softly. "Yes. Thank you. I'm all right now."

She relaxed against me. So beautiful, so dainty a creature.

Larry leaned toward us. "You're better now?"

"Yes."

"That's fine. You'll be all right. Don't think about it."

He was convinced she was insane. I breathed again the vague hope that it might not be so. She was huddled against me. Her face, upturned to mine, had color in it now; red lips; a faint rose tint in the pale cheeks.

She murmured, "Is this New York?"

My heart sank. "Yes," I answered. "Of course it is."

"But when?"

"What do you mean?"

"I mean, what year?"

"Why, 1935!"

She caught her breath. "And your name is—"

"George Rankin."

"And I,"—her laugh had a queer break in it—"I am Mistress Mary Atwood. But just a few minutes ago—oh, am I dreaming? Surely I'm not insane!"

Larry again leaned over us. "What are you talking about?"

"You're friendly, you two. Like men; strange, so very strange-looking young men. This—this carriage without any horses—I know now it won't hurt me."

She sat up. "Take me to your doctor. And then to the general of your army. I must see him, and warn him. Warn you all." She was turning half hysterical again. She laughed wildly. "Your general—he won't be General Washington, of course. But I must warn him."

She gripped me. "You think I am demented. But I am not. I am Mary Atwood, daughter of Major Charles Atwood, of General Washington's staff. That was my home, where you broke the window. But it did not look like that a few moments ago. You tell me this is the year 1935, but just a few moments ago I was living in the year 1777!"

CHAPTER II

From Out of the Past

"Sane?" said Dr. Alten. "Of course she's sane." He stood gazing down at Mary Atwood. He was a tall, slim fellow, this famous young alienist, with dark hair turning slightly grey at the temples and a neat black mustache that made him look older than he was. Dr. Alten at this time, in spite of his eminence, had not yet turned forty.

"She's sane," he reiterated. "Though from what you tell me, it's a wonder that she is." He smiled gently at the girl. "If you don't mind, my dear, tell us just what happened to you, as calmly as you can."

She sat by an electrolier in Dr. Alten's living room. The yellow light gleamed on her white satin dress, on her white shoulders, her beautiful face with its little round black beauty patch, and the curls of the white wig dangling to her neck. From beneath the billowing, flounced skirt the two satin points of her slippers showed.

A beauty of the year 1777! This thing so strange! I gazed at her with quickened pulse. It seemed that I was dreaming; that as I sat before her in my tweed business suit with its tubular trousers I was the anachronism! This should have been candle-light illumining us; I should have been a powdered and bewigged gallant, in gorgeous satin and frilled shirt to match her dress. How strange, how futuristic we three men of 1935 must have looked to her! And this city through which we had whirled her in the throbbing taxi—no wonder she was overwrought.

Alten fumbled in the pockets of his dressing gown for cigarettes. "Go ahead, Miss Mary. You are among friends. I promise we will try and understand."

She smiled. "Yes. I—I believe you." Her voice was low. She sat staring at the floor, choosing her words carefully; and though she stumbled a little, her story was coherent. Upon the wings of her words my fancy conjured that other Time-world, more than a hundred and fifty years ago.

"I was at home to-night," she began. "To-night after dinner. I have no relatives except my father. He is General Washington's aide. We live—our home is north of the city. I was alone, except for the servants.

"Father sent word to-night that he was coming to see me. The messenger got through the British lines. But the redcoats are everywhere. They were quartered in our house. For months I have been little more than a servant to a dozen of My Lord's Howe's officers. They are gentlemen, though: I have no complaint. Then they left, and father, knowing it, wanted to come to see me.

"He should not have tried it. Our house is watched. He promised me he would not wear the British red." She shuddered. "Anything but that—to have him executed as a spy. He would not risk that, but wear merely a long black cloak.

"He was to come about ten o'clock. But at midnight there was no sign of him. The servants were asleep. I sat alone, and every pounding hoof-beat on the road matched my heart.

"Then I went into the garden. There was a dim moon in and out of the clouds. It was hot, like to-night. I mean, why it *was* to-night. It's so strange—"

In the silence of Alten's living room we could hear the hurried ticking of his little mantle clock, and from the street outside came the roar of a passing elevated train and the honk of a taxi. This was New York of 1935. But to me the crowding ghosts of the past were here. In fancy I saw the white pillars of the moonlit Atwood home. A garden with a dirt road beside it. Red-coated British soldiers passing.... And to the south the little city of New York extending northward from crooked Maiden Lane and the Bowling Green....

"Go on, Mistress Mary."

"I sat on a bench in the garden. And suddenly before me there was a white ghost. A shape. A wraith of something which a moment before had not been there. I sat too frightened to move. I could not call out. I tried to, but the sound would not come.

"The shape was like a mist, a little ball of cloud in the center of the garden lawn. Then in a second or two it was solid—a thing like a shining cage, with crisscrossing white bars. It was like a room; a metal cage like a room. I thought that the thing was a phantom or that I was asleep and dreaming. But it was real."

Alten interrupted. "How big was it?"

"As large as this room; perhaps larger. But it was square, and about twice as high as a man."

A cage, then, some twenty feet square and twelve feet high.

She went on: "The cage door opened. I think I was standing, then, and I tried to run but could not. The—the *thing* came from the door of the cage and walked toward me. It was about ten feet tall. It looked—oh, it looked like a man!"

She buried her face in her hands. Again the room was silent. Larry was seated, staring at her; all of us were breathless.

"Like a man?" Alten prompted gently.

"Yes; like a man." She raised her white face. This girl out of the past! Admiration for her swept me anew—she was bravely trying to smile.

- 40 -

"Like a man. A thing with legs, a body, a great round head and swaying arms. A jointed man of metal! You surely must know all about them."

"A Robot!" Larry muttered.

"You have them here, I suppose. Like that rumbling carriage without horses, this jointed iron man came walking toward me. And it spoke! A most horrible hollow voice—but it seemed almost human. And what it said I do not know, for I fainted. I remember falling as it came walking toward me, with stiff-jointed legs.

"When I came to my senses I was in the cage. Everything was humming and glowing. There was a glow outside the bars like a moonlit mist. The iron monster was sitting at a table, with peculiar things—mechanical things—"

"The controls of the cage-mechanisms," said Alten. "How long were you in the cage?"

"I don't know. Time seemed to stop. Everything was silent except the humming noises. They were everywhere. I guess I was only half conscious. The monster sat motionless. In front of him were big round clock faces with whirling hands. Oh, I suppose you don't find this strange; but to me—!"

"Could you see anything outside the cage?" Alten persisted. "No. Just a fog. But it was crawling and shifting. Yes!—I remember now—I could not see anything out there, but I had the thought, the feeling, that there were tremendous things to see! The monster spoke again and told me to be careful; that we were going to stop. Its iron hands pulled at levers. Then the humming grew fainter; died away; and I felt a shock.

"I thought I had fainted again. I could just remember being pulled through the cage door. The monster left me on the ground. It said, 'Lie there, for I will return very soon.'

"The cage vanished. I saw a great cliff of stone near me; it had yellow-lighted openings, high up in the air. And big stone fences hemmed me in. Then I realized I was in an open space between a lot of stone houses. One towered like a cliff, or the side of a pyramid—"

"The back yard of that house on Patton Place!" Larry exclaimed. He looked at me. "Has it any back yard, George?"

"How should I know?" I retorted. "Probably has."

"Go on," Alten was prompting.

"That is nearly all. I found a doorway leading to a dark room. I crawled through it toward a glow of light. I passed through another room. I thought

I was in a nightmare, and that this was my home. I remembered that the cage had not moved. It had hardly lurched. Just trembled; vibrated.

"But this was not my home. The rooms were small and dark. Then I peered through a window on a strange stone street. And saw these strange-looking young men. And that is all—all I can tell you."

She had evidently held herself calm by a desperate effort. She broke down now, sobbing without restraint.

CHAPTER III

Tugh, the Cripple

The portals of this mystery had swung wide to receive us. The tumbling events which menaced all our world of 1935 were upon us now. A maelstrom. A torrent in the midst of which we were caught up like tiny bits of cork and whirled away.

But we thought we understood the mystery. We believed we were acting for the best. What we did was no doubt ill-considered; but the human mind is so far from omniscient! And this thing was so strange!

Alten said, "You have a right to be overwrought, Mistress Mary Atwood. But this thing is as strange to us as it is to you. I called that iron monster a Robot. But it does not belong to our age: if it does I have never seen one such as you describe. And traveling through Time—"

He smiled down at her. "That is not a commonplace everyday occurrence to us, I assure you. The difference is that in this world of ours we can understand—or at least explain—these things as being scientific. And so they have not the terror of the supernatural."

Mary was calmer now. She returned his smile. "I realize that; or at least I am trying to realize it."

What a level-headed girl was this! I touched her arm. "You are very wonderful—"

Alten brushed me away. "Let's try and reduce it to rationality. The cage was— is, I should say, since of course it still exists—that cage is a Time-traveling vehicle. It is traveling back and forth through Time, operated by a Robot. Call it that. A pseudo-human monster fashioned of metal in the guise of a man."

Even Alten had to force himself to speak calmly, as he gazed from one to the other of us. "It came, no doubt from some future age, where half-human mechanisms are common, and Time-traveling is known. That cage probably does not travel in Space, but only in Time. In the future—somewhere—the

Space of that house on Patton Place may be the laboratory of a famous scientist. And in the past—in the year 1777—that same Space was the garden of Mistress Atwood's home. So much is obvious. But why—"

"Why," Larry burst out, "did that iron monster stop in 1777 and abduct this girl?"

"And why," I intercepted, "did it stop here in 1935?" I gazed at Mary. "And it told you it would return?"

"Yes."

Alten was pondering. "There must be some connection, of course.... Mistress Mary, had you never seen this cage before?"

"No."

"Nor anything like it? Was anything like that known to your Time?"

"No. Oh, I cannot truly say that. Some people believe in phantoms, omens and witchcraft. There was in Salem, in the Massachusetts Colony, not so many years ago—"

"I don't mean that. I mean Time-traveling."

"There were soothsayers and fortune-tellers, and necromancers with crystals to gaze into the future."

"We still have them," Alten smiled. "You see, we don't know much more than you do about this thing."

I said, "Did you have any enemy? Anyone who wished you harm?"

She thought a moment. "No—yes, there was one." She shuddered at the memory. "A man—a cripple—a horribly repulsive man of about one score and ten years. He lives down near the Battery." She paused.

"Tell us about him," Larry urged.

She nodded. "But what could he have to do with this? He is horribly deformed. Thin, bent legs, a body like a cask and a bulging forehead with goggling eyes. My Lord Howe's officers say he is very intelligent and very learned. Loyal to the King, too. There was a munitions plot in the Bermudas, and this cripple and Lord Howe were concerned in it. But Father likes the fellow and says that in reality he wishes our cause well. He is rich.

"But you don't want to hear all this. He—he made love to me, and I repulsed him. There was a scene with Father, and Father had our lackeys throw him out. That was a year ago. He cursed horribly. He vowed then that some day he—he would have me; and get revenge on Father. But he has kept away. I have not seen him for a twelvemonth."

We were silent. I chanced to glance at Alten, and a strange look was on his face.

He said abruptly, "What is this cripple's name, Mistress Mary?"

"Tugh. He is known to all the city as Tugh. Just that. I never heard any Christian name."

Alten rose sharply to his feet. "A cripple named Tugh?"

"Yes," she affirmed wonderingly. "Does it mean anything to you?"

Alten swung on me. "What is the number of that house on Patton Place? Did you happen to notice?"

I had, and wondering I told him.

"Just a minute," he said. "I want to use the phone."

He came back to us in a moment: his face was very solemn. "That house on Patton Place is owned by a man named Tugh! I just called a reporter friend; he remembers a certain case: he confirmed what I thought. Mistress Mary, did this Tugh in your Time ever consult doctors, trying to have his crippled body made whole?"

"Why, of course he did. I have heard that many times. But his crippled, deformed body cannot be cured."

Alten checked Larry and me when we would have broken in with astonished questions. He said:

"Don't ask me what it means; I don't know. But I think that this cripple—this Tugh—has lived both in 1777 and 1935, and is traveling between them in this Time-traveling cage. And perhaps he is the human master of that Robot."

Alten made a vehement gesture. "But we'd better not theorize; it's too fantastic. Here is the story of Tugh in our Time. He came to me some three years ago; in 1932, I think. He offered any price if I could cure his crippled body. All the New York medical fraternity knew him. He seemed sane, but obsessed with the idea that he must have a body like other men. Like Faust, who, as an old man, paid the price of his soul to become youthful, he wanted to have the beautiful body of a young man."

Alten was speaking vehemently. My thoughts ran ahead of his words; I could imagine with grewsome fancy so many things. A cripple, traveling to different ages seeking to be cured. Desiring a different body....

Alten was saying, "This fellow Tugh lived alone in that house on Patton Place. He was all you say of him, Mistress Mary. Hideously repulsive. A sinister personality. About thirty years old.

"And, in 1932, he got mixed up with a girl who had a somewhat dubious reputation herself. A dancer, a frequenter of night-clubs, as they used to be called. Her name was Doris Johns—something like that. She evidently thought she could get money out of Tugh. Whatever it was, there was a big uproar. The girl had him arrested, saying that he had assaulted her. The police had quite a time with the cripple."

Larry and I remembered a few of the details of it now, though neither of us had been in New York at the time.

Alten went on: "Tugh fought with the police. Went berserk. I imagine they handled him pretty roughly. In the Magistrate's Court he made another scene, and fought with the court attendants. With ungovernable rage he screamed vituperatives, and was carried kicking, biting and snarling from the court-room. He threatened some wild weird revenge upon all the city officials— even upon the city itself."

"Nice sort of chap," Larry commented.

But Alten did not smile. "The Magistrate could only hold him for contempt of Court. The girl had absolutely no evidence to support her accusation of assault. Tugh was finally dismissed. A week later he murdered the girl.

"The details are unimportant; but he did it. The police had him trapped in his house; had the house surrounded—this same one on Patton Place—but when they burst in to take him, he had inexplicably vanished. He was never heard from again."

Alten continued to regard us with grim, solemn face. "Never heard from— until to-night. And now we hear of him. How he vanished, with the police guarding every exit to that house—well, it's obvious, isn't it? He went into another Time-world. Back to 1777, doubtless."

Mary Atwood gave a little cry. "I had forgotten that I must warn you. Tugh told me once, before Father and I quarreled with him, that he had a mysterious power. He was a most wonderful man, he said. And there was a world in the future—he mentioned 1934 or 1935—which he hated. A great city whose people had wronged him; and he was going to bring death to them. Death to them all! I did not heed him. I thought he was demented, raving...."

Alten's little clock ticked with tumultuous heartbeat through another silence. The great city around us, even though this was two o'clock in the morning, throbbed with a myriad of blended sounds.

A warning! Was the girl from out of the past giving us a warning of coming disaster to this great city?

Alten was pacing the floor. "What are we to do—tell the authorities? Take Mistress Mary Atwood to Police Headquarters and inform them that she has come from the year 1777? And that, if we are not careful, there will be an attack upon New York?"

"No!" I burst out. I could fancy how we would be received at Police Headquarters if we did that! And our pictures in to-morrow's newspapers. Mary's picture, with a jibing headline ridiculing us.

"No," echoed Alten. "I have no intention of doing it. I'm not so foolish as that." He stopped before Mary. "What do you want to do? You're obviously an exceptionally intelligent, level-headed girl. Heaven knows you need to be."

"I—I want to get back home," she stammered.

A pang shot through me as she said it. A hundred and fifty years to separate us. A vast gulf. An impassible barrier.

"That mechanism said it would return!"

"Exactly," agreed Alten. An excitement was upon us all. "Exactly what I mean! Shall we chance it? Try it? There's nothing else I can think of to do. I have a revolver and two hunting rifles."

"Just what do you mean?" I demanded.

"I mean, we'll take my car and go to Tugh's house on Patton Place. Right now! And if that mechanical monster returns, we'll seize it!"

Alten, the usually calm, precise man of science, was tensely vehement. "Seize it! Why not? Three of us, armed, ought to be able to overcome a Robot! Then we'll seize the Time-traveling cage. Perhaps we can operate it. If not, with it in our possession we'll at least have something to show the authorities; there'll be no ridicule then!"

Our inescapable destiny was making us plunge so rashly into this mystery! With the excitement and the strange fantasy of it upon us, we thought we were acting for the best.

Within a quarter of an hour, armed and with a long overcoat and a scarf to hide Mary Atwood's beauty, we took Alten's car and drove to Patton Place.

CHAPTER IV

The Fight With the Robot

Patrolman McGuire quite evidently had not passed through Patton Place since we left it; or at least he had not noticed the broken window. The house appeared as before, dark, silent, deserted, and the broken basement window yawned with its wide black opening.

"I'll leave the car around on the other street," Alten said as slowly we passed the house. "Quick—no one's in sight; you three get out here."

We crouched in the dim entryway and in a moment he joined us.

I clung to Mary Atwood's arm. "You're not afraid?" I asked.

"No. Yes; of course I am afraid. But I want to do what we planned. I want to go back to my own world, to my Father."

"Inside!" Alten whispered. "I'll go first. You two follow with her."

I can say now that we should not have taken her into that house. It is so easy to look back upon what one might have done!

We climbed through the window, into the dark front basement room. There was only silence, and our faintly padding footsteps on the carpeted floor. The furniture was shrouded with cotton covers standing like ghosts in the gloom. I clutched the loaded rifle which Alten had given me. Larry was similarly armed; and Alten carried a revolver.

"Which way, Mary?" I whispered. "You're sure it was outdoors?"

"Yes. This way, I think."

We passed through the connecting door. The back room seemed to be a dismantled kitchen.

"You stay with her here, a moment," Alten whispered to me. "Come on, Larry. Let's make sure no one—nothing—is down here."

I stood silent with Mary, while they prowled about the lower floor.

"It may have come and gone," I whispered.

"Yes." She was trembling against me.

It seemed to me an eternity while we stood there listening to the faint footfalls of Larry and Alten. Once they must have stood quiet; then the silence leaped and crowded us. It is horrible to listen to a pregnant silence which every moment might be split by some weird unearthly sound.

Larry and Alten returned. "Seems to be all clear," Alten whispered. "Let's go into the back yard."

The little yard was dim. The big apartment house against its rear wall loomed with a blank brick face, save that there were windows some eight stories up. Only a few windows overlooked this dim area with its high enclosing walls. The space was some forty feet square, and there was a faded grass plot in the center.

We crouched near the kitchen door, with Mary behind us in the room. She said she could recall the cage having stood near the center of the yard, with its door facing this way....

Nearly an hour passed. It seemed that the dawn must be near, but it was only around four o'clock. The same storm clouds hung overhead—a threatening storm which would not break. The heat was oppressing.

"It's come and gone," Larry whispered; "or it isn't coming. I guess that this—"

And then it came! We were just outside the doorway, crouching against the shadowed wall of the house. I had Mary close behind me, my rifle ready.

"There!" whispered Alten.

We all saw it—a faint luminous mist out near the center of the yard—a crawling, shifting ball of fog.

Alten and Larry, one on each side of me, shifted sidewise, away from me. Mary stood and cast off her dark overcoat. We men were in dark clothes, but she stood in gleaming white against the dark rectangle of doorway. It was as we had arranged. A moment only, she stood there; then she moved back, further behind me in the black kitchen.

And in that moment the cage had materialized. We were hoping its occupant had seen the girl, and not us. A breathless moment passed while we stared for the first time at this strange thing from the Unknown.... A formless, glowing mist, it quickly gathered itself into solidity. It seemed to shrink. It took form. From a wraith of a cage, in a second it was solid. And so silently, so swiftly, came this thing out of Time into what we call the Present! The dim yard a second ago had been empty.

The cage stood there, a thing of gleaming silver bars. It seemed to enclose a single room. From within its dim interior came a faint glow, which outlined something standing at the bars, peering out.

The doorway was facing us. There had been utter silence; but suddenly, as though to prove how solid was this apparition, we heard the clank of metal, and the door slid open.

I turned to make sure that Mary was hiding well behind me. The way back to the street, if need for escape arose, was open to her.

I turned again, to face the shining cage. In the doorway something stood peering out, a light behind it. It was a great jointed thing of dark metal some ten feet high. For a moment it stood motionless. I could not see its face clearly, though I knew there was a suggestion of human features, and two great round glowing spots of eyes.

It stepped forward—toward us. A jointed, stiff-legged step. Its arms were dangling loosely; I heard one of its mailed hands clank against its sides.

"Now!" Alten whispered.

I saw Alten's revolver leveling, and my own rifle went up.

"Aim at its face," I murmured.

We pulled our triggers together, and two spurts of flame spat before us. But the thing had stooped an instant before, and we missed. Then came Larry's shot. And then chaos.

I recall hearing the ping of Larry's bullet against the mailed body of the Robot. At that it crouched, and from it leaped a dull red-black beam of light. I heard Mary scream. She had not fled but was clinging to me. I cast her off.

"Run! Get back! Get away!" I cried.

Larry shouted, as we all stood bathed in the dull light from the Robot.

"Look out! It sees us!"

He fired again, into the light—and murmured, "Why—why—"

A great surprise and terror was in his tone. Beside me, with half-leveled revolver, Alten stood transfixed. And he too was muttering something.

All this happened in an instant. And there I was aware that I was trying to get my rifle up for firing again; but I could not. My arms stiffened. I tried to take a step, tried to move a foot, but could not. I was rooted there; held, as though by some giant magnet, to the ground!

This horrible dull-red light! It was cold—a frigid, paralyzing blast. The blood ran like cold water in my veins. My feet were heavy with the weight of my body pressing them down.

Then the Robot was moving; coming forward; holding the light upon us. I thought I heard its voice—and a horrible, hollow, rasping laugh.

My brain was chilling. I had confused thoughts; impressions, vague and dreamlike. As though in a dream I felt myself standing there with Mary clinging to me. Both of us were frozen inert upon our feet.

I tried to shout, but my tongue was too thick; my throat seemed swelling inside. I heard Alten's revolver clatter to the stone pavement of the yard. And saw him fall forward—out.

I felt that in another instant I too would fall. This damnable, chilling light! Then the beam turned partly away, and fell more fully upon Larry. With his youth and greater strength than Alten's or mine, he had resisted its first blast. His weapon had fallen; now he stooped and tried to seize it; but he lost his balance and staggered backward against the house wall.

And then the Robot was upon him. It sprang—this mechanism!—this machine in human form! And, with whatever pseudo-human intelligence actuated its giant metal body, it reached under Larry for his rifle! Its great mailed hand swept the ground, seized the rifle and flung it away. And as Larry twisted sidewise, the Robot's arm with a sweep caught him and rolled him across the yard. When he stopped, he lay motionless.

I heard myself thickly calling to Mary, and the light flashed again upon us. And then we fell forward. Clinging together, we fell....

I did not quite lose consciousness. It seemed that I was frozen, and drifting off half into a nightmare sleep. Great metal arms were gathering Mary and me from the ground. Lifting us; carrying us....

We were in the cage. I felt myself lying on the grid of a metal floor. I could vaguely see the crossed bars of the ceiling overhead, and the latticed walls around me....

Then the dull-red light was gone. The chill was gone. I was warming. The blessed warm blood again was coursing through my veins, reviving me, bringing back my strength.

I turned over, and found Mary lying beside me. I heard her softly murmur:

"George! George Rankin!"

The giant mechanism clanked the door closed, and came with stiff, stilted steps back into the center of the cage. I heard the hollow rumble of its voice, chuckling, as its hand pulled a switch.

At once the cage-room seemed to reel. It was not a physical movement, though, but more a reeling of my senses, a wild shock to all my being.

Then, after a nameless interval, I steadied. Around me was a humming, glowing intensity of tiny sounds and infinitely small, infinitely rapid vibrations. The whole room grew luminous. The Robot, seated now at a table, showed for a moment as thin as an apparition. All this room—Mary lying beside me, the mechanism, myself—all this was imponderable, intangible, unreal.

And outside the bars stretched a shining mist of movement. Blurred shifting shapes over a vast illimitable vista. Changing things; melting landscapes. Silent, tumbling, crowding events blurred by our movement as we swept past them.

We were traveling through Time!

CHAPTER V

The Girl from 2930

I must take up now the sequence of events as Larry saw them. I was separated from Larry during most of the strange incidents which befell us later; but from his subsequent account of what happened to him I am constructing several portions of this history, using my own words based upon Larry's description of the events in which I personally did not participate; I think that this method avoids complications in the narrative and makes more clear my own and Larry's simultaneous actions.

Larry recovered consciousness in the back yard of the house on Patton Place probably only a moment or two after Mary and I had been snatched away in the Time-traveling cage. He found himself bruised and battered, but apparently without injuries. He got to his feet, weak and shaken. His head was roaring.

He recalled what had happened to him, but it seemed like a dream. The back yard was then empty. He remembered vaguely that he had seen the mechanism carry Mary and me into the cage, and that the cage had vanished.

Larry knew that only a few moments had passed. The shots had aroused the neighborhood. As he stood now against the house wall, dizzily looking around, he was aware of calling voices from the nearby windows.

Then Larry stumbled over Alten, who was lying on his face near the kitchen doorway. Still alive, he groaned as Larry fell over him; but he was unconscious.

Forgetting all about his weapon, Larry's first thought was to rush out for help. He staggered through the dark kitchen into the front room, and through the corridor into the street.

Patton Place, as before, was deserted. The houses were dark; the alarm was all in the rear. There were no pedestrians, no vehicles, and no sign of a policeman. Dawn was just coming; as Larry turned eastward he saw, in a patch of clearing sky, stars paling with the coming daylight.

With uncertain steps, out in the middle of the street, Larry ran eastward through the middle of the street, hoping that at the next corner he might encounter someone, or find a telephone over which he might call the police.

But he had not gone more than five hundred feet when suddenly he stopped; stood there wavering, panting, staring with whirling senses. Near the middle of the street, with the faint dawn behind it, a ball of gathering mist had appeared directly in his path. It was a luminous, shining mist—and it was gathering into form!

In seconds a small, glowing cage of white luminous bars stood there in the street, where there had just been nothing! It was not the Time-traveling cage from the house yard he had just left. No—he knew it was not that one. This one was similar, but much smaller.

The shock of its appearance held Larry for a moment transfixed. It had so silently, so suddenly appeared in his path that Larry was now within a foot or two of its doorway.

The doorway slid open, and a man leaped out. Behind him, a girl peered from the doorway. Larry stood gaping, wholly confused. The cage had materialized so abruptly that the leaping man collided with him before either man could avoid the other. Larry gripped the man before him; struck out with his fists and shouted. The girl in the doorway called frantically:

"Harl-no noise! Harl-stop him!"

Then, suddenly the two of them were upon Larry and pulling him toward the doorway of the cage. Inside, he was jerked; he shouted wildly; but the girl slammed the door. Then in a soft, girlish voice, in English with a curiously indescribable accent and intonation, the girl said hastily:

"Hold him, Harl! Hold him! I'll start the traveler!"

The black garbed figure of a slim young man was gripping Larry as the girl pulled a switch and there was a shock, a reeling of Larry's senses, as the cage, motionless in Space, sped off into Time....

It seems needless to encumber this narrative with prolonged details of how Larry explained himself to his two captors. Or how they told him who they were; and from whence they had come; and why. To Larry it was a fantastic—and confusing at first—series of questions and answers. An hour? The words have no meaning. They were traveling through Time. Years were minutes—the words meaning nothing save how they impressed the vehicle's human occupants. To them all it was an interval of mutual distrust which was gradually changing into friendship. Larry found the two strangers singularly direct; singularly forceful in quiet, calm fashion; singularly keen of perception. They had not meant to capture him. The encounter had startled them, and Larry's shouts would have brought others upon the scene.

Almost at once they knew Larry was no enemy, and told him so. And in a moment Larry was pouring out all that had happened to him; and to Alten and Mary Atwood and me. This strange thing! But to Larry now, telling it to these strange new companions, it abruptly seemed not fantastic, but only sinister. The Robot, an enemy, had captured Mary Atwood and me, and whirled us off in the other—the larger—cage.

And in this smaller cage Larry was with friends—for he suddenly found their purpose the same as his! They were chasing this other Time-traveler, with its semi-human, mechanical operator!

The young man said, "You explain to him, Tina. I will watch."

He was a slim, pale fellow, handsome in a queer, tight-lipped, stern-faced fashion. His close-fitting black silk jacket had a white neck ruching and white cuffs; he wore a wide white-silk belt, snug black-silk knee-length trousers and black stockings.

And the girl was similarly dressed. Her black hair was braided and coiled upon her head, and ornaments dangled from her ears. Over her black blouse was a brocaded network jacket; her white belt, compressing her slim waist, dangled with tassels; and there were other tassels on the garters at the knees of her trousers.

She was a pale-faced, beautiful girl, with black brows arching in a thin line, with purple-black eyes like somber pools. She was no more than five feet tall, and slim and frail. But, like her companion, there was about her a queer aspect of calm, quiet power and force of personality—physical vitality merged with an intellect keenly sharp.

She sat with Larry on a little metal bench, listening, almost without interruption, to his explanation. And then, succinctly she gave her own. The young man, Harl, sat at his instruments, with his gaze searching for the other cage, five hundred feet away in Space, but in Time unknown.

And outside the shining bars Larry could vaguely see the blurred, shifting, melting vistas of New York City hastening through the changes Time had brought to it.

This young man, Harl, and this girl, Tina, lived in New York City in the Time-world of 2930 A. D. To Larry it was a thousand years in the future. Tina was the Princess of the American Nation. It was an hereditary title, non-political, added several hundred years previously as a picturesque symbol. A tradition; something to make less prosaic the political machine of Republican government. Tina was loved by her people, we afterward came to learn.

Harl was an aristocrat of the New York City of Tina's Time-world, a scientist. In the Government laboratories, under the same roof where Tina dwelt, Harl had worked with another, older scientist, and—so Tina told me—together they had discovered the secret of Time-traveling. They had built two cages, a large and a small, which could travel freely through Time.

The smaller vehicle—this one in which Larry now was speeding—was, in the Time-world of 2930, located in the garden of Tina's palace. The other, somewhat larger, they had built some five hundred feet distant, just beyond the palace walls, within a great Government laboratory.

Harl's fellow scientist—the leader in their endeavors, since he was much older and of wider experience—was not altogether trusted by Tina. He took the credit for the discovery of Time-traveling; yet, said Tina, it was Harl's genius which in reality had worked out the final problems.

And this older scientist was a cripple. A hideously repulsive fellow, named Tugh!

"Tugh!" exclaimed Larry.

"The same," said Tina in her crisp fashion. "Yes—undoubtedly the same. So you see why what you have told us was of such interest. Tugh is a Government leader in our world; and now we find he has lived in *your* Time, and in the Time of this Mary Atwood."

From his seat at the instrument table, Harl burst out: "So he murdered a girl of 1935, and has abducted another of 1777? You would not have me judge him, Tina—"

"No one," she said, "may judge without full facts. This man here—this Larry of 1935—tells us that only a mechanism is in the larger cage—which is what we thought, Harl. And this mechanism, without a doubt, is the treacherous Migul."

There was, in 2930, a vast world of machinery. The god of the machine had developed them to almost human intricacy. Almost all the work of the world, particularly in America, and most particularly in the mechanical center of New York City, was done by machinery. And the machinery itself was guided, handled, operated—even, in some instances, constructed—by other, more intricate machines. They were fashioned in pseudo-human form— thinking, logically acting, independently acting mechanisms: the Robots. All but human, they were—a new race. Inferior to humans, yet similar.

And in 2930 the machines, slaves of idle human masters, had been developed too highly! They were upon the verge of a revolt!

All this Tina briefly sketched now to Larry. And to Larry it seemed a very distant, very academic danger. Yet so soon all of us were plunged into the midst of it!

The revolt had not yet come, but it was feared. A great Robot named Migul seemed fomenting it. The revolt was smouldering; at any moment it would burst; and then the machines would rise to destroy the humans.

This was the situation when Harl and Tugh completed the Time-traveling vehicles in this world. They had been tested, but never used. Then Tugh had vanished; was gone now; and the larger of the two vehicles was also gone.

Both Harl and Tina had always distrusted Tugh. They thought him allied to the Robots. But they had no proof; and suavely he denied it, and helped always with the Government activities struggling to keep the mechanical slaves docile and at work.

Tugh and the larger vehicle had vanished, and so had Migul, the insubordinate, giant mechanism—at which, unknown to the Government officials, Tina and Harl had taken the other cage and started in pursuit. It was possible that Tugh was loyal; that Migul had abducted him and stolen the cage.

"Wait!" exclaimed Larry. "I'm trying to figure this out. It seems to hang together. It almost does, but not quite. When did Tugh vanish from your world?"

"To our consciousness," Tina answered, "about three hours ago. Perhaps a little longer than that."

"But look here," Larry protested: "according to my story and that of Mary Atwood, Tugh lived in 1935 and in 1777 for three years."

Confusing? But in a moment Larry understood it. Tugh could have taken the cage, gone to 1777 and to 1935, alternated between them for what was to him, and to those Time-worlds, three years—then have returned to 2930 *on the same day of his departure.* He would have lived these three years; grown that much older; but to the Time-world of 2930 neither he nor the cage would have been missed.

"That," said Tina, "is what doubtless he did. The cage is traveling again. But you, Larry, tell us only Migul is in it."

"I couldn't say that of my own knowledge," said Larry. "Mary Atwood said so. It held only the mechanism you call Migul. And now Migul has with him Mary and my friend George Rankin. We must reach them."

"We want that quite as much as you do," said Harl. "And to find Tugh. If he is a friend we must save him; if a traitor—punish him."

Larry began, "But can you get to the other cage?"

"Only if it stops," said Tina. "*When* it stops, I should say."

"Come here," said Harl. "I will show you."

Larry crossed the glowing room. He had forgotten its aspect—the ghostly unreality around him. He too—his body, like Harl's and Tina's—was of the same wraith-like substance.... Then, suddenly, Larry's viewpoint shifted. The room and its occupants were real and tangible. And outside the glowing bars—everything out there was the unreality.

"Here," said Harl. "I will show you. It is not visible yet."

Each of the cages was equipped with an intricate device, strange of name, which Larry and I have since termed a Time-telespectroscope. Larry saw it now as a small metal box, with tuning vibration dials, batteries, coils, a series of tiny prisms and an image-mirror—the whole surmounted by what appeared the barrel of a small telescope. Harl had it leveled and was gazing through it.[1]

[1] The workings of the Time-telespectroscope involve all the intricate postulates and mathematical formulae of Time-traveling itself. As a matter of practicality, however, the results obtained are simple of understanding. The etheric vibratory rate of the vehicles while traveling through Time was

constantly changing. Through the telespectroscope one cage was visible to the other across the five hundred feet of intervening Space when they approached a simultaneous Time; when they, so to speak, were tuned in unison.

Thus, Harl explained, the other cage would show as a ghost, the faintest of wraiths, over a Time-distance of some five or ten years. And the closer in Time they approached it, the more solid it would appear.

The enemy cage was not visible, now. But Harl and Tina had glimpsed it on several occasions. What vast realms Time opens within a single small segment of Space! The larger vehicle seemed speeding back and forth. A dash into the year 1777! as Larry learned from Mary Atwood.

And there had been several evidences of the cage halting in 1935. Larry's account explained two such pauses. But the others? Those others, which brought to the City of New York such amazing disaster? We did not learn of them until much later. But Alten lived through them, and presently I shall reconstruct them from his account.

The larger cage was difficult to trace in its sweep along the corridors of Time. Never once had Tina and Harl been able to stop simultaneously with it, for a year has so many separate days and hours. The nearest they came was the halt in the night of June 8-9, when they encountered Larry, and, startled, seized him and moved on again.

Harl continued to gaze through the eyepiece of the detecting instrument. But nothing showed, and the mirror-grid on the table was dark.

"But—which way are we going?" Larry stammered.

"Back," said Tina. "The retrograde.... Wait! Do not do that!"

Larry had turned toward where the bars, less luminous, showed a dark rectangle like a window. The desire swept him to gaze out at the shining, changing scene.

But Tina checked him. "Do not do that! Not yet! It is too great a shock in the retrograde. It was to me."

"But where are we?"

In answer she gestured toward a series of tiny dials on the table edge. There were at least two score of them, laid in a triple bank. Dials to record the passing minutes, hours, days; the years, the centuries! Larry stared at the small whirring pointers. Some were a blur of swift whirling movement—the hours and days. Tina showed Larry how to read them. The cage was passing through the year 1880. In a few moments of Larry's consciousness it was 1799. Then 1793. The infant American nation was here now. But with the cage retrograding, soon they would be in the Revolutionary War.

Tina said. "The other cage may go back to 1777, if Tugh meant ill to Mary Atwood, or wants revenge upon her father, at you said. We shall see."

They had reached 1790 when Harl gave a low ejaculation.

"You see it?" Tina murmured.

"Yes. Very faintly."

Larry bent tensely forward. "Will it show on the mirror?"

"Yes; presently. We are about ten years from it. If we get closer, the mirror will show it."

But the mirror held dark. No—now it was glowing a trifle. A vague luminosity.

Tina moved toward the instrument controls nearby. "Watch closely, Harl. I will slow us down."

It seemed to Larry that the humming with which everything around him was endowed, now began descending in pitch. And his head suddenly was unsteady. A singular, wild, queer feeling was within him. An unrest. A tugging torment of every tiny cell of his body.

Tina said. "Hold steady, Larry, for when we stop."

"Will it shock me?"

"Yes—at first. But the shock will not harm you: it is nearly all mental."

The mirror held an image now—the other cage. Larry saw, on the six-inch square mirror surface, a crawling, melting scene of movement. And in the midst of it, the image of the other cage, faint and spectral. In all the mirrored movement, only the apparition of the cage was still. And this marked it; made it visible.

Over an interval, while Larry stared, the ghostly image grew plainer. They were approaching its Time-factor!

"It is stopping," Harl murmured. Larry was aware that he had left the eyepiece and joined Tina at the controls.

"Tina, let us try to get it right this time."

"Yes."

"In 1777; but which month, would you say?"

"It has stopped! See?"

Larry heard them clicking switches, and setting the controls for a stop. Then he felt Tina gently push him.

"Sit here. Standing, you might fall."

He found himself on a bench. He could still see the mirror. The ghost of the other cage was now lined more plainly upon it.

"This month," said Tina, setting a switch. "Would not you say so? And this day."

"But the hour, Tina? The minute?"

The vast intricate corridors of Time!

"It would be in the night. Hasten, Harl, or we will pass! Try the night— around midnight. Even Migul has the mechanical intelligence to fear a daylight pausing."

The controls were set for the stop. Larry heard Tina murmuring, "Oh, I pray we may have judged with correctness!"

The vehicle was rapidly coming to a stop. Larry gripped the table, struggling to hold firm to his reeling senses. This soundless, grinding halt! His swaying gaze strayed from the mirror. Outside the glowing bars he could now discern the luminous greyness separating. Swift, soundless claps of light and dark, alternating. Daylight and darkness. They had been blended, but now they were separating. The passing, retrograding days—a dozen to the second of Larry's consciousness. Then fewer. Vivid daylight. Black night. Daylight again.

"Not too slowly, Harl; we will be seen!... Oh, it is gone!"

Larry saw the mirror go blank. The image on it had flared to great distinctness, faded, and was gone. Darkness was around Larry. Then daylight. Then darkness again.

"Gone!" echoed Harl's disappointed voice. "But it stopped here!... Shall we stop, Tina?"

"Yes! Leave the control settings as they are. Larry—be careful, now."

A dragging second of grey daylight. A plunge into night. It seemed to Larry that all the universe was soundlessly reeling. Out of the chaos, Tina was saying:

"We have stopped. Are you all right, Larry?"

"Yes," he stammered.

He stood up. The cage room, with its faint lights, benches and settles, instrument tables and banks of controls, was flooded with moonlight from outside the bars. Night, and the moon and stars out there.

Harl slid the door open. "Come, let us look."

The reeling chaos had fallen swiftly from Larry. With Tina's small black and white figure beside him, he stood at the threshold of the cage. A warm gentle night breeze fanned his face.

A moonlit landscape lay somnolent around the cage. Trees were nearby. The cage stood in a corner of a field by a low picket fence. Behind the trees, a ribbon of road stretched away toward a distant shining river. Down the road some five hundred feet, the white columns of a large square brick house gleamed in the moonlight. And behind the house was a garden and a group of barns and stables.

The three in the cage doorway stood whispering, planning. Then two of them stepped to the ground. They were Larry and Tina; Harl remained to guard the cage.

The two figures on the ground paused a moment and then moved cautiously along the inside line of the fence toward the home of Major Atwood. Strange anachronisms, these two prowling figures! A girl from the year 2930; a man from 1935!

And this was revolutionary New York, now. The little city lay well to the south. It was open country up here. The New York of 1935 had melted away and was gone....

This was a night in August of 1777.

CHAPTER VI

The New York Massacre of 1935

Dr. Alten recovered consciousness in the back yard of the house on Patton Place just a few moments after Larry had encountered the smaller Time-traveling cage and been carried off by Harl and Tina. Previously to that, of course, the mysterious mechanism in the guise of a giant man had abducted Mary Atwood and me in the larger Time-cage.

Alten became aware that people were bending over him. The shots we had taken at the Robot had aroused the neighborhood. A policeman arrived.

The sleeping neighbors had heard the shots, but it seemed that none had seen the cage, or the metal man who had come from it. Alten said nothing. He was taken to the nearest police station where grudgingly, he told his story. He was laughed at; reprimanded for alcoholism. Evidently, according to the police sergeant, there had been a fight, and Alten had drawn the loser's end. The police confiscated the two rifles and the revolver and decided that no one but Alten had been hurt. But at best it was a queer affair. Alten had not been shot; he was just stiff with cold; he said a dull-red ray had fallen upon him and stiffened him with its frigid blast. Utter nonsense!

Dr. Alten was a man of standing. It was a reprehensible affair, but he was released upon his own recognizance. He was charged with breaking into the untenanted home of one Tugh; of illegally possessing firearms; of disturbing the peace—a variety of offenses all rational to the year 1935.

But Alten's case never reached even its hearing in the Magistrate's Court. He arrived home just after dawn, that June 9, still cold and stiff from the effects of the ray, and bruised and battered by the sweeping blow of Miguel's great iron arm. He recalled vaguely seeing Larry fall, and the iron monster bearing Mary Atwood and me away. What had happened to Larry, Alten could not guess, unless the Robot had returned, ignored him and taken his friend away.

During that day of June 9 Alten summoned several of his scientific friends, and to them he told fully what had happened to him. They listened with a keen understanding and a rational knowledge of the possibility that what he said was true; but credibility they could not give him.

The noon papers came out.

NOTED ALIENIST ATTACKED BY GHOST Felled by One of the Fantastic Monsters of His Brain

A jocular, jibing account. Then Alten gave it up. He had about decided to plead guilty in the Magistrate's Court to disorderly conduct and all the rest of it! That was preferable to being judged a liar, or insane.

And then, at about 9 P.M. on the evening of June 9, the first of the mechanical monsters came stalking from the house on Patton Place—the beginning of the revenge which Tugh had threatened when arrested. The policeman at the corner—one McGuire—turned in the first hysterical alarm. He rushed into a little candy and stationery store shouting that he had seen a piece of machinery running wild. His telephone call brought a squad of his comrades. The Robot at first did no damage.

McGuire later told how he saw it as it emerged from the entryway of the Tugh house. It came lurching out into the street—a giant thing of dull grey metal, with tubular, jointed legs; a body with a great bulging chest; a round head, eight or ten feet above the pavement; eyes that shot fire.

The policeman took to his heels. There was a commotion in Patton Place during those next few minutes. Pedestrians saw the thing standing in the middle of the street, staring stupidly around it. The head wobbled. Some said that the eyes shot fire; others, that it was not the eyes, but more like a torch in its mailed hand. The torch shot a small beam of light around the street—a beam which was dull-red.

The pedestrians fled. Their cries brought people to the nearby house windows. Women screamed. Presently bottles were thrown from the windows. One of these crashed against the iron shoulder of the monster. It turned its head: as though its neck were rubber, some said. And it gazed upward, with a human gesture as though it were not angry, but contemptuous.

But still, beyond a step or two in one direction or another, it merely stood and waved its torch. The little dull-red beam of light carried no more than twenty or thirty feet. The street in a few moments was clear of pedestrians; remained littered with glass from the broken bottles. A taxi came suddenly around the corner, and the driver, with an almost immediate tire puncture, saw the monster. He hauled up to the curb, left his cab and ran.

The Robot saw the taxicab, and stood gazing. It turned its torch-beam on it, and seemed surprised that the thing did not move. Then thinking evidently that this was a less cowardly enemy than the humans, it made a rush to it. The chauffeur had not turned off his engine when he fled, so the cab stood throbbing.

The Robot reached it; cuffed it with a huge mailed fist. The windshield broke; the windows were shattered; but the cab stood purring, planted upon its four wheels.

Strange encounter! They say that the Robot tried to talk to it. At last, exasperated, it stepped backward, gathered itself and pounced on it again. Stooping, it put one of its great arms down under the wheels, the other over the hood, and with prodigious strength heaved the cab into the air. It crashed on its side across the street, and in a moment was covered with flames.

It was about this time that Patrolman McGuire came back to the scene. He shot at the monster a few times; hit it, he was sure. But the Robot did not heed him.

The block was now in chaos. People stood at most of the windows, crowds gathered at the distant street corners, while the blazing taxicab lighted the block with a lurid glare. No one dared approach within a hundred feet or so of the monster. But when, after a time, it showed no disposition to attack, throngs at every distinct point of vantage tried to gather where they could see it. Those nearest reported back that its face was iron; that it had a nose, a wide, yawning mouth, and holes for eyes. There were certainly little lights in the eye-holes.

A small, fluffy white dog went dashing up to the monster and barked bravely at its heels. It leaped nimbly away when the Robot stooped to seize it. Then, from the Robot's chest, the dull-red torch beam leaped out and down. It caught the little dog, and clung to it for an instant. The dog stood transfixed; its bark turned to a yelp; then a gurgle. In a moment it fell on its side; then lay motionless with stiffened legs sticking out.

All this happened within five minutes. McGuire's riot squad arrived, discreetly ranged itself at the end of the block and fired. The Robot by then had retreated to the entryway of the Tugh house, where it stood peering as though with curiosity at all this commotion. There came a clanging from the distance: someone had turned in a fire alarm. Through the gathered crowds and vehicles the engines came tearing up.

Presently there was not one Robot, but three: a dozen! More than that, many reports said. But certain it is that within half an hour of the first alarm, the block in front of Tugh's home held many of the iron monsters. And there were many human bodies lying strewn there, by then. A few policemen had made a stand at the corner, to protect the crowd against one of the Robots. The thing had made an unexpected infuriated rush....

There was a panic in the next block, when a thousand people suddenly tried to run. A score of people were trampled under foot. Two or three of the Robots ran into that next block—ran impervious to the many shots which now were fired at them. From what was described as slots in the sides of their iron bodies they drew swords—long, dark, burnished blades. They ran, and at each fallen human body they made a single stroke of decapitation, or, more generally, cut the body in half.

The Robots did not attack the fire engines. Emboldened by this, firemen connected a hose and pumped a huge jet of water toward the Tugh house. The Robots then rushed it. One huge mechanism—some said it was twelve feet tall—ran heedlessly into the firemen's high-pressure stream, toppled backward from the force of the water and very strangely lay still. Killed? Rather, out of order: deranged: it was not human, to be killed. But it lay motionless, with the fire hose playing upon it. Then abruptly there was an explosion. The fallen Robot, with a deafening report and a puff of green flame, burst into flying metallic fragments like shrapnel. Nearby windows were broken from the violent explosion, and pieces of the flying metal were hurled a hundred feet or more. One huge chunk, evidently a plate of the thing's body, struck into the crowd two blocks away, and felled several people.

At this smashing of one of the mechanisms, its brother Robots went for the first time into aggressive action. A hundred or more were pouring now from the vacant house of the absent Tugh....

The alarm by ten o'clock had spread throughout the entire city. Police reserves were called out, and by midnight soldiers were being mobilized. Panics were starting everywhere. Millions of people crowded in on small Manhattan Island, in the heart of which was this strange enemy.

Panics.... Yet human nature is very strange. Thousands of people started to leave Manhattan, but there were other thousands during that first skirmish who did their best to try and get to the neighborhood of Patton Place to see what was going on. They added greatly to the confusion. Traffic soon was stalled everywhere. Traffic officers, confused, frightened by the news which was bubbled at them from every side, gave wrong orders; accidents began to occur. And then, out of the growing confusion, came tangles, until, like a dammed stream, all the city mid-section was paralyzed. Vehicles were abandoned everywhere.

Reports of what was happening on Patton Place grew more confused. The gathering nearby crowds impeded the police and firemen. The Robots, by ten o'clock, were using a single great beam of dull-red light. It was two or three feet broad. It came from a spluttering, hissing cylinder mounted on runners which the Robots dragged along the ground, and the beam was like that of a great red searchlight. It swung the length of Patton Place in both directions. It hissed against the houses; penetrated the open windows which now were all deserted; swept the front cornices of the roofs, where crowds of tenants and others were trying to hide. The red beam drove back the ones near the edge, except those who were stricken by its frigid blast and dropped like plummets into the street, where the Robots with flashing blades pounced upon them.

Frigid was the blast of this giant light-beam. The street, wet from the fire-hose, was soon frozen with ice—ice which increased under the blast of the beam, and melted in the warm air of the night when the ray turned away.

From every distant point in the city, awed crowds could see that great shaft when it occasionally shot upward, to stain the sky with blood.

Dr. Alten by midnight was with the city officials, telling them what he could of the origin of this calamity. They were a distracted group indeed! There were a thousand things to do, and frantically they were giving orders, struggling to cope with conditions so suddenly unprecedented. A great city, millions of people, plunged into conditions unfathomable. And every moment growing worse. One calamity bringing another, in the city, with its myriad diverse activities so interwoven. Around Alten the clattering, terrifying reports were surging. He sat there nearly all that night; and near dawn, an official plane carried him in a flight over the city.

The panics, by midnight, were causing the most deaths. Thousands, hundreds of thousands, were trying to leave the island. The tube trains, the subways, the elevateds were jammed. There were riots without number in them. Ferryboats and bridges were thronged to their capacity. Downtown Manhattan, fortunately comparatively empty, gave space to the crowds plunging down from the crowded foreign quarters bordering Greenwich Village. By dawn it was estimated that five thousand people had been trampled to death by the panics in various parts of the city, in the tubes beneath the rivers and on departing trains.

And another thousand or more had been killed by the Robots. How many of these monstrous metal men were now in evidence, no one could guess. A hundred—or a thousand. The Time-cage made many trips between that night of June 9 and 10, 1935, and a night in 2930. Always it gauged its return to this same night.

The Robots poured out into Patton Place. With running, stiff-legged steps, flashing swords, small light-beams darting before them, they spread about the city....

CHAPTER VII

The Vengeance of Tugh

A myriad individual scenes of horror were enacted. Metal travesties of the human form ran along the city streets, overturning stalled vehicles, climbing into houses, roaming dark hallways, breaking into rooms.

There was a woman who afterward told that she crouched in a corner, clutching her child, when the door of her room was burst in. Her husband, who had kept them there thinking it was the safest thing to do, fought futilely with the great thing of iron. Its sword slashed his head from his body with a single stroke. The woman and the little child screamed, but the monster ignored them. They had a radio, tuned to a station in New Jersey which was broadcasting the events. The Robot seized the instrument as though in a frenzy of anger, tore it apart, then rushed from the room.

No one could give a connected picture of the events of that horrible night. It was a series of disjointed incidents out of which the imagination must construct the whole.

The panics were everywhere. The streets were stalled with traffic and running, shouting, fighting people. And the area around Greenwich Village brought reports of continued horror.

The Robots were of many different forms; some pseudo-human; others, great machines running amuck—things more monstrous, more horrible even, than those which mocked humanity. There was a great pot-bellied monster which forced its way somehow to a roof. It encountered a crouching woman and child in a corner of the parapet, seized them, one in each of its great iron hands, and whirled them out over the housetops.

———————————

By dawn it seemed that the Robots had mounted several projectors of the giant red beam on the roofs of Patton Place. They held a full square mile, now, around Tugh's house. The police and firemen had long since given up fighting them. They were needed elsewhere—the police to try and cope with the panics, and the firemen to fight the conflagrations which everywhere began springing up. Fires, the natural outcome of chaos; and fires, incendiary—made by criminals who took advantage of the disaster to fatten like ghouls upon the dead. They prowled the streets. They robbed and murdered at will.

The giant beams of the Robots carried a frigid blast for miles. By dawn of that June 10th, the south wind was carrying from the enemy area a perceptible wave of cold even as far as Westchester. Allen, flying over the city, saw the devastated area clearly. Ice in the streets—smashed vehicles— the gruesome litter of sword-slashed human bodies. And other human bodies, plucked apart; strewn....

Alten's plane flew at an altitude of some two thousand feet. In the growing daylight the dark prowling figures of the metal men were plainly seen. There were no humans left alive in the captured area. The plane dropped a bomb into Washington Square where a dozen or two of the Robots were gathered. It missed them. The plane's pilot had not realized that they were grouped around a projector; its red shaft sprang up, caught the plane and clung to it. Frigid blast! Even at that two thousand feet altitude, for a few seconds Alten and the others were stiffened by the cold. The motor missed; very nearly stopped. Then an intervening rooftop cut off the beam, and the plane escaped.

All this I have pictured from what Dr. Alten subsequently told me. He leaves my narrative now, since fate hereafter held him in the New York City of 1935. But he has described for me three horrible days, and three still more horrible nights. The whole world now was alarmed. Every nation offered its forces of air and land and sea to overcome these gruesome invaders. Warships steamed for New York harbor. Soldiers were entrained and brought to the city outskirts. Airplanes flew overhead. On Long Island, Staten Island, and in New Jersey, infantry, tanks and artillery were massed in readiness.

But they were all very nearly powerless to attack. Manhattan Island still was thronged with refugees. It was not possible for the millions to escape; and for the first day there were hundreds of thousands hiding in their homes. The city could not be shelled. The influx of troops was hampered by the outrush of civilians.

By the night of the tenth, nevertheless, ten thousand soldiers were surrounding the enemy area. It embraced now all the mid-section of the island. The soldiers rushed in. Machine-guns were set up.

But the Robots were difficult to find. With this direct attack they began fighting with an almost human caution. Their bodies were impervious to bullets, save perhaps in the orifices of the face which might or might not be vulnerable. But when attacked, they skulked in the houses, or crouched like cautious animals under the smashed vehicles. Then there were times when they would wade forward directly into machine-gun fire—unharmed— plunging on until the gunners fled and the Robots wreaked their fury upon the abandoned gun.

The only hand-to-hand conflicts took place on the afternoon of June 10th. A full thousand soldiers were killed—and possibly six or eight of the Robots. The troops were ordered away after that; they made lines across the island to the north and to the south, to keep the enemy from increasing its area. Over Greenwich Village now, the circling planes—at their highest altitude, to avoid the upflung crimson beams—dropped bombs. Hundreds of houses there were wrecked. Tugh's house could not be positively identified, though the attack was directed at it most particularly. Afterward, it was found by chance to have escaped.

The night of June 10th brought new horrors. The city lights failed. Against all the efforts of the troops and the artillery fire which now was shelling the Washington Square area, the giant mechanisms pushed north and south. By midnight, with their dull-red beams illumining the darkness of the canyon streets, they had reached the Battery, and spread northward beyond the northern limits of Central Park.

It is estimated that by then there were still a million people on Manhattan Island.

The night of the 11th, the Robots made their real attack. Those who saw it, from planes overhead, say that upon a roof near Washington Square a machine was mounted from which a red beam sprang. It was not of parallel rays, like the others; this one spread. And of such power it was, that it painted the leaden clouds of the threatening, overcast night. Every plane, at whatever high altitude, felt its frigid blast and winged hastily away to safety.

Spreading, dull-red beam! It flashed with a range of miles. Its light seemed to cling to the clouds, staining like blood; and to cling to the air itself with a dull lurid radiance.

It was a hot night, that June 11th, with a brewing thunderstorm. There had been occasional rumbles of thunder and lightning flashes. The temperature was perhaps 90° F.

Then the temperature began falling. A million people were hiding in the great apartment houses and homes of the northern sections, or still struggling to escape over the littered bridges or by the paralyzed transportation systems—and that million people saw the crimson radiance and felt the falling temperature.

80°. Then 70°. Within half an hour it was at 30°! In unheated houses, in midsummer, in the midst of panic, the people were swept by chilling cold. With no adequate clothing available they suffered greatly—and then abruptly they were freezing. Children wailing with the cold; then asleep in numbed, last slumber....

Zero weather in midsummer! And below zero! How cold it got, there is no one to say. The abandoned recording instrument in the Weather Bureau was found, at 2:16 A.M., the morning of June 12, 1935, to have touched minus 42° F.

The gathering storm over the city burst with lightning and thunder claps through the blood-red radiance. And then snow began falling. A steady white downpour, a winter blizzard with the lightning flashing above it, and the thunder crashing.

With the lightning and thunder and snow, crazy winds sprang up. They whirled and tossed the thick white snowflakes; swept in blasts along the city streets. It piled the snow in great drifts against the houses; whirled and sucked it upward in white powdery geysers.

At 2:30 A.M. there came a change. The dull-red radiance which swept the city changed in color. Through the shades of the spectrum it swung up to violet. And no longer was it a blast of cold, but of heat! Of what inherent temperature the ray of that spreading beam may have been, no one can say. It caught the houses, and everything inflammable burst into flame. Conflagrations were everywhere—a thousand spots of yellow-red flames, like torches, with smoke rolling up from them to mingle with the violet glow overhead.

The blizzard was gone. The snow ceased. The storm clouds rolled away, blasted by the pendulum winds which lashed the city.

By 3 A.M. the city temperature was over 100° F—the dry, blistering heat of a midsummer desert. The northern city streets were littered with the bodies of people who had rushed from their homes and fallen in the heat, the wild winds and the suffocating smoke outside.

And then, flung back by the abnormal winds, the storm clouds crashed together overhead. A terrible storm, born of outraged nature, vent itself on the city. The fires of the burning metropolis presently died under the torrent of falling water. Clouds of steam whirled and tossed and hissed close overhead, and there was a boiling hot rain.

By dawn the radiance of that strange spreading beam died away. The daylight showed a wrecked, dead city. Few humans indeed were left alive on Manhattan that dawn. The Robots and their apparatus had gone....

The vengeance of Tugh against the New York City of 1935 was accomplished.

(To be continued.)

Arthur J. Burks'
MANAPE THE MIGHTY
Is Coming Soon!

Just as the terrific unknown force reached its apex, she stepped
across the plate.

HELL'S DIMENSION

By Tom Curry

Professor Lambert deliberately ventures into a Vibrational Dimension to join his fiancee in its magnetic torture-fields.

"Now, Professor Lambert, tell us what you have done with the body of your assistant Miss Madge Crawford. Her car is outside your door, has stood there since early yesterday morning. There are no footprints leading away from the house and you can't expect us to believe that an airplane picked her off the roof. It will make it a lot easier if you tell us where she is. Her parents are greatly worried about her. When they telephoned, you refused to talk to them, would not allow them to speak to Miss Crawford. They are alarmed as to her fate. While you are not the sort of man who would injure a young woman, still, things look bad for you. You had better explain fully."

John Lambert, a man of about thirty-six, tall, spare, with black hair which was slightly tinged with gray at the temples in spite of his youth, turned large eyes which were filled with agony upon his questioners.

Lambert was already internationally famous for his unique and astounding experiments in the realm of sound and rhythm. He had been endowed by one of the great electrical companies to do original work, and his laboratory, in which he lived, was situated in a large tract of isolated woodland some forty miles from New York City. It was necessary for the success of his work that as few disturbing noises as possible be made in the neighborhood. Many of his experiments with sound and etheric waves required absolute quiet and freedom from interrupting noises. The delicate nature of some of the machines he used would not tolerate so much as the footsteps of a man within a hundred yards, and a passing car would have disrupted them entirely.

Lambert was terribly nervous; he trembled under the gaze of the stern detective, come with several colleagues from a neighboring town at the call of Madge Crawford's frightened family. The girl, whose picture stood on a working table nearby, looked at them from the photograph as a beautiful young woman of twenty-five, light of hair, with large eyes and a lovely face.

Detective Phillips pointed dramatically to the likeness of the missing girl. "Can you," he said, "look at her there, and deny you loved her? And if she did not love you in return, then we have a motive for what you have done— jealousy. Come, tell us what you have done with her. Our men will find her, anyway; they are searching the cellar for her now. You can't hope to keep her, alive, and if she is dead—"

Lambert uttered a cry of despair, and put his face in his long fingers. "She—she—don't say she's dead!"

"Then you did love her!" exclaimed Phillips triumphantly, and exchanged glances with his companions.

"Of course I love her. And she returned my love. We were secretly engaged, and were to be married when we had finished these extremely important experiments. It is infamous though, to accuse me of having killed her; if I have done so, then it was no fault of mine."

"Then you did kill her?"

"No, no. I cannot believe she is really gone."

"Why did you evade her parents' inquiries?"

"Because ... I have been trying to bring her ... to re-materialize her."

"You mean to bring her back to life?"

"Yes."

"Couldn't a doctor do that better than you, if she is hidden somewhere about here?" asked Phillips gravely.

"No, no. You do not understand. She cannot be seen, she has dematerialized. Oh, go away. I'm the only man, save, possibly, my friend Doctor Morgan, who can help her now. And Morgan—I've thought of calling him, but I've been working every instant to get the right combination. Go away, for God's sake!"

"We can't go away until we have found out Miss Crawford's fate," said Phillips patiently.

Another sleuth entered the immense laboratory. He made his way through the myriad strange machines, a weird collection of xylophones, gongs, stone slabs cut in peculiar patterns to produce odd rhythmic sounds, electrical apparatus of all sorts. Near Phillips was a plate some feet square, of heavy metal, raised from the floor on poles of a different substance. About the ceiling were studs thickly set of the same sort of metal as was the big plate.

One of the sleuths tapped his forehead, pointing to Lambert as the latter nervously lighted a cigarette.

The newcomer reported to Phillips. He held in his hand two or three sheets of paper on which something was written.

"The only other person here is a deaf mute," said the sleuth to Phillips, his superior. "I've got his story. He writes that he takes care of things, cooks their meals and so on. And he writes further that he thinks the woman and this guy Lambert were in love with each other. He has no idea where she has gone to. Here, you read it."

Phillips took the sheets and continued: "'Yesterday morning about ten o'clock I was passing the door of the laboratory on my way to make up Professor Lambert's bed. Suddenly I noticed a queer, shimmering, greenish-blue light streaming down from the walls and ceiling of the laboratory. I was right outside the place and though I cannot hear anything, I was knocked down and I twisted and wriggled around like a snake. It felt like something with a thousand little paws but with great strength was pushing me every way. When there was a lull, and the light had stopped for a few moments, I staggered to my feet and ran madly for my own quarters, scared out of my head. As I went by the kitchen, I saw Miss Crawford at the sink there, filling some vases and arranging flowers as she usually did every morning.

"'If she called to me, I did not hear her or notice her lips moving. I believe she came to the door.

"'I was going to quit, when I recovered myself, angry at what had occurred; but then, I began to feel ashamed for being such a baby, for Professor Lambert has been very good to me. About fifteen minutes after I went to my room, I was able to return to the kitchen. Miss Crawford was not there, though the flowers and vases were. Then, as I started to work, still a little alarmed, Professor Lambert came rushing into the kitchen, an expression of terror on his face. His mouth was open, and I think he was calling. He then ran out, back to the laboratory, and I have not seen Miss Madge since. Professor Lambert has been almost continuously in the work-room since then, and—I kept away from it, because I was afraid.'"

Two more members of Phillips' squad broke into the laboratory and came toward the chief. They had been working at physical labor, for they were still perspiring and one regarded his hands with a rueful expression.

"Any luck?" asked Phillips eagerly.

"No, boss. We been all over the place, and we dug every spot we could get to earth in the cellar. Most of it's three-inch concrete, without a sign of a break."

"Did you look in the furnace?"

"We looked there the first thing. She ain't there."

There were several closets in the laboratory, and Phillips opened all of them and inspected them. As he moved near the big plate, Lambert uttered a cry of warning. "Don't disturb that, don't touch anything near it!"

"All right, all right," said Phillips testily.

The skeptical sleuths had classified Lambert as a "nut," and were practically sure he had done away with Madge Crawford because she would not marry him.

Still, they needed better evidence than their mere beliefs. There was no corpus delicti, for instance.

"Gentlemen," said Lambert at last, controlling his emotions with a great effort. "I will admit to you that I am in trepidation and a state of mental torture as to Miss Crawford's fate. You are delaying matters, keeping me from my work."

"He thinks about work when the girl he claims he loves has disappeared," said Doherty, in a loud whisper to Phillips. Doherty was one of the sleuths who had been digging in the cellar, and the hard work had made his temper short.

"You must help us find Miss Crawford before we can let you alone," said Phillips. "Can't you understand that you are under grave suspicion of having injured her, hidden her away? This is a serious matter, Professor Lambert. Your experiments can wait."

"This one cannot," shouted Lambert, shaking his fists. "You are fools!"

"Steady now," said Doherty.

"Perhaps you had better come with us to the district attorney's office," went on Phillips. "There you may come to your senses and realize the futility of trying to cover up your crime—if you have committed one. If you have not, why do you not tell us where Miss Crawford is?"

"Because I do not know myself," replied Lambert. "But you can't take me away from here. I beg of you, gentlemen, allow me a little more time. I must have it."

Phillips shook his head. "Not unless you tell us logically what has occurred," he said.

"Then I must, though I do not think you will comprehend or even believe me. Briefly, it is this: yesterday morning I was working on the final series of experiments with a new type of harmonic overtones plus a new type of sinusoidal current which I had arranged with a series of selenium cells. When I finally threw the switch—remember, I was many weeks preparing the apparatus, and had just put the final touches on early that morning—there was a sound such as never had been heard before by human ears, an indescribable sound, terrifying and mysterious. Also, there was a fierce, devouring verditer blue light, and this came from the plates and studs you see, but so great was its strength that it got out of control and leaped about the room like a live thing. For some moments, while it increased in intensity as I raised the power of the current by means of the switch I held in my hand, I watched and listened in fascination. My instruments had ceased to record, though they are the most delicate ever invented and can handle almost anything which man can even surmise."

The perspiration was pouring from Lambert's face, as he recounted his story. The detectives listened, comprehending but a little of the meaning of the scientist's words.

"What has this to do with Miss Crawford?" asked Doherty impatiently.

Phillips held up his hand to silence the other sleuth. "Let him finish," he ordered. "Go on, professor."

"The sensations which I was undergoing became unendurable," went on Lambert, in a low, hoarse voice. "I was forced to cry out in pain and confusion.

"Miss Crawford evidently heard my call, for a few moments later, just as the terrific unknown force reached its apex, she dashed into the laboratory, and stepped across the plate you see there.

"I was powerless. Though I shut off the current by a superhuman effort, she—she was gone!"

Lambert put his face in his hands, a sob shook his broad shoulders.

"Gone?" repeated Phillips. "What do you mean, gone?"

"She disappeared, before my very eyes," said the professor shakily. "Torn into nothingness by the fierce force of the current or sound. Since then, I have been trying to reproduce the conditions of the experiment, for I wish to bring her back. If I cannot do so, then I want to join her, wherever she has gone. I love her, I know now that I cannot possibly live without her. Will you please leave me alone, now, so that I can continue?"

Doherty laughed derisively. "What a story," he jeered.

"Keep quiet, Doherty," ordered Phillips. "Now, Professor Lambert, your explanation of Miss Crawford's disappearance does not sound logical to us, but still we are willing to give you every chance to bring her back, if what you say is true. We cannot leave you entirely alone, because you might try to escape or you might carry out your threat of suicide. Therefore, I am going to sit over there in the corner, quietly, where I can watch you but will not interfere with your work. We will give you until midnight to prove your story. Then you must go with us to the district attorney. Do you agree to that?"

Lambert nodded, eagerly. "I agree. Let me work in peace, and if I do not succeed then you may take me anywhere you wish. If you can," he added, in an undertone.

Doherty and the others, at Phillips' orders, filed from the laboratory. "One thing more, professor," said Phillips, when they were alone and the professor was preparing to work. "How do you explain the fact, if your story is true, that Miss Crawford was killed and made to disappear, while you yourself, close by, were uninjured?"

"Do you see these garments?" asked Lambert, indicating some black clothes which lay on a bench nearby. "They insulated me from the current and partially protected me from the sound. Though the force was very great, great enough to penetrate my insulation, it was handicapped in my case because of the garments."

"I see. Well, you may go on."

Phillips moved in the chair he had taken, from time to time. He could hear the noises of his men, still searching the premises for Madge Crawford, and Professor Lambert heard them, too.

"Will you tell your men to be quiet?" he cried at last.

There were dark circles under Lambert's eyes. He was working in a state of feverish anxiety. When the girl he loved had dematerialized from under his very eyes, panic had seized him; he had ripped away wires to break the current and lost the thread of his experiment, so that he could not reproduce it exactly without much labor.

The scientist put on the black robes, and Phillips wished he too had some protective armor, even though he did believe that Lambert had told them a parcel of lies. The deaf mute's story was not too reassuring. Phillips warned his companions to be more quiet, and he himself sat quite still.

Lambert knew that the sleuths thought he was stark mad. He was aware of the fact that he had but a few hours in which to save the girl who had come at his cry to help him, who had loved him and whom he loved, only to be torn into some place unknown by the forces which were released in his experiment. And he knew he would rather die with her than live without her.

He labored feverishly, though he tried to keep his brain calm in order to win. His notes helped him up to a certain point, but when he had made the final touches he had not had time to bring the data up to the moment, being eager to test out his apparatus. It was while testing that the awful event had occurred and he had seen Madge Crawford disappear before his very eyes.

Her eyes, large and frightened, burned in his mind.

The deaf mute, Felix, a small, spare man of about fifty, sent the professor some food and coffee through one of the sleuths. Lambert swallowed the coffee, but waved away the rest, impatiently. Phillips, watching his suspect constantly, was served a light supper at the end of the afternoon.

There seemed to be a million wires to be touched, tested, and various strange apparatus. Several times, later on in the evening. Lambert threw the big switch with an air of expectancy, but little happened. Then Lambert would go to work again, testing, testing—adjusting this and that till Phillips swore under his breath.

"Only an hour more, professor," said Phillips, who was bored to death and cramped from trying to obey the professor's orders to keep still. A circle of cigarette-ends surrounded the sleuth.

"Only an hour," agreed Lambert. "Will you please be quiet, my man? This is a matter of my fiancée's life or death."

Phillips was somewhat disgruntled, for he felt he had done Lambert quite a favor in allowing him to remain in the laboratory for so long, to prove his story.

"I wish Doctor Morgan were here; I ought to have sent for him, I suppose," said Lambert, a few minutes later. "Will you allow me to get him? I cannot seem to perfect this last stage."

"No time, now," declared Phillips. "I said till midnight."

It was obvious to Lambert that the detective had become certain during the course of the evening that the scientist was mad. The ceaseless fiddling and the lack of results or even spectacular sights had convinced Phillips that he had to do with a crank.

"I think I have it now," said Lambert coolly.

"What?" asked Phillips.

"The original combination. I had forgotten one detail in the excitement, and this threw me off. Now I believe I will succeed—in one way or another. I warn you, be careful. I am about to release forces which may get out of my control."

"Well, now, don't get reckless," begged Phillips nervously. The array of machines had impressed him, even if Lambert did seem a fool.

"You insist upon remaining, so it is your own risk," said Lambert coolly.

Lambert, in the strange robes, was a bizarre figure. The hood was thrown back, exposing his pale, black-bearded face, the wan eyes with dark circles under them, and the twitching lips.

"If you find yourself leaving this vale of tears," went on the scientist, ironically, to the sleuth, "you will at least have the comfort of realizing that as the sound-force disintegrates your mortal form you are among the first of men to be attuned to the vibrations of the unknown sound world. All matter is vibration; that has been proven. A building of bricks, if shaken in the right manner, falls into its component parts; a bridge, crossed by soldiers in certain rhythmic time, is torn from its moorings. A tuning fork, receiving the sound vibrations from one of a similar size and shape begins to vibrate in turn. These are homely analogies, but applied to the less familiar sound vibrations, which make up our atomic world, they may help you to understand how the terrific forces I have discovered can disintegrate flesh."

The scientist looked inquiringly at Phillips. As the sleuth did not move, but sat with folded arms, Lambert shrugged and said, "I am ready."

Lambert raised his hood, and Phillips said, in a spirit of bravado, "You can't scare me out of here."

"Here goes the switch," cried Lambert.

He made the contact, as he had before. He stood for a moment, and this time the current gained force. The experimenter pushed his lever all the way over.

A terrible greenish-blue light suddenly illuminated the laboratory, and through the air there came sound vibrations which seemed to tear at Phillips' body. He found himself on the floor, knocked from his chair, and he writhed this way and that, speechless, suffering a torment of agony. His whole flesh seemed to tremble in unison with the waves which emanated from the machines which Lambert manipulated.

After what seemed hours to the suffering sleuth, the force diminished, and soon Phillips was able to rise. Trembling, the detective cursed and yelled for help in a high-pitched voice.

Lambert had thrown back his hood, and was rocking to and fro in agony.

"Madge, Madge," he cried, "what have I done! Come back to me, come back!"

Doherty and the others came running in at their chief's shouts. "Arrest him," ordered Phillips shakily. "I've stood enough of this nonsense."

The detectives started for Lambert. He saw them coming, and swiftly threw off the protective garments he wore.

"Stand back!" he cried, and threw the switch all the way over. The verditer green light smashed through the air, and the queer sound sensations smacked and tore them; Doherty, who had drawn a revolver when he was answering Phillips' cries, fired the gun into the air, and the report seemed to battle with the vibrating ether.

Lambert, as he threw the switch, leaped forward and landed on the metal plate under the ceiling studs, in the very center of the awful disturbance and unprotected from its force.

For a few moments, Lambert felt racking pain, as though something were tearing at his flesh, separating the very atoms. The scientist saw the wriggling figures of the sleuths, in various strange positions, but his impressions were confused. His head whirled round and round, he swayed to and fro, and, finally, he thought he fell down, or rather, that he had melted, as a lump of sugar dissolves in water.

"He's gone—gone—"

In the heart of nothingness was Lambert, his body torn and racked in a shrieking chaos of sound and a blinding glare of iridescent light which seemed too much to bear.

His last conscious thought was a prayer, that, having failed to bring back his sweetheart, Madge Crawford, he was undergoing a step toward the same destination to which he had sent her.

John Lambert came to with a shudder. But it was not a mortal shudder. He could sense no body; had no sense of being confined by matter. He was in a strange, chilly place—a twilight region, limitless, without dimensions.

Yet he could feel something, in an impersonal way, vaguely indifferent. He had no pain now.

He was moving, somehow. He had one impelling desire, and that was to discover Madge Crawford. Perhaps it was this thought which directed his movements.

Intent upon finding the girl, if she was indeed in this same strange world that he was, he did not notice for some time—how long, he had no way of telling—that there were other beings which tried to impede his progress. But as he grew more accustomed to the unfamiliar sensations he was undergoing, he found his path blocked again and again by queer beings.

They were living, without doubt, and had intelligence, and evinced hostility toward him. But they were shapeless, shapeless as amoebas. He heard them in a sort of soundless whisper, and could see them without the use of eyes. And he shuddered, though he could feel no body in which he might be confined. Still, when he pinched viciously with invisible fingers at the spot where his face should have been, a twinge of pain registered on the vague consciousness which appeared to be all there was to him.

He was not sure of his substance, though he could evidently experience human sensations with his amorphous body. He did not know whether he could see; yet, he was dodging this way and that, as the beings who occupied this world tried to stop him.

They gave him the impression of gray shapes, and in coppery shadows things gleamed and closed in on him.

He seemed to hear a cry, and he knew that he was receiving a call for help from Madge Crawford. He tried to run, pushed determinedly toward the spot, impelled by his love for the girl.

Now, as he hurried, he occasionally was stopped short by collision with the formless shapes which were all about him. He was hampered by them, for they followed him, making a sound like wind heard in a dream. Whatever medium he was in was evidently thickly inhabited by the hostile beings who claimed this world as their own. Though he could not actually feel the medium, he could sense that it was heavy. He leaped and ran, fighting his way through the increasing hosts, and the roar of their voice-impressions increased in his consciousness.

Yet there seemed to be nothing, nothing tangible save vagueness. He felt he was in a blind spot in space, a place of no dimensions, no time, where beings abhorred by nature, things which had never developed any dimensional laws, existed.

The cry for help struck him, with more force this time. Lambert, whatever form he was in, realised that he was close to the end of his journey to Madge Crawford.

He tried to speak, and had the impression that he said something reassuring. He then bumped into some vibrational being which he knew was Madge. His ears could not hear, nor could his flesh feel, but his whole form or cerebrum sensed he held the woman he loved in his arms.

And she was speaking to him, in accents of fear, begging him to save her.

"John, John, you have come at last. They have been torturing me terribly. Save me."

"Darling Madge, I will do everything I can. Now I have found you, and we are together and will never part. Can you hear me?"

"I know what you are thinking, and what you wish to say. I can't exactly hear; it all seems vague, and impossible. Yet I can suffer. They have been hitting me with something which makes me shudder and shake—there, they are at it again."

Lambert felt the sensations, now, which the girl had made known to him. He felt crowded by gray beings, and his existence was troubled by spasms of pain-impressions. He knew Madge was crying out, too.

He could not comprehend the attacks, or guess their meaning. But the situation was unendurable.

Anger shook him, and he began to fight, furiously but vaguely. They were closely hemmed in, but when Lambert began to strike out with hands and legs, the beings gave way a little. The scientist tried to shout, and though he could actually hear nothing, the result was gratifying. The formless creatures seemed to scatter and draw back in confusion as he yelled his defiance.

"They hate that," Madge said to him. "I have screamed myself hoarse and that is why they have not killed me—if I can be killed."

"I do not believe we can. But they can torture us," replied Lambert. "It is an everlasting half-life or quarter-life, and these creatures who call this Hell's Dimension home, have nothing but hatred for us in their consciousness."

The inhabitants of the imperfect world had closed in once again and the sharp instruments of torture they used were being thrust into the invisible bodies of the two humans. Each time, Lambert was unable to restrain his cries, for it seemed that he was being torn to pieces by vibrations.

He yelled until he could not speak above a whisper, or at least until the impressions of speech he gave forth did not trouble the beings. The two humans, still bound to some extent by their mortal beliefs, were chivvied to and fro, and struck and bullied. The creatures seemed to delight in this sport.

The two felt they could not die; yet they could suffer terribly. Would this go on through eternity? Was there no release?

They were trying to tear Madge away from him. She was fighting them, and Lambert, in a frenzy of rage, made a determined effort to get away with the girl from their tormentors.

They retreated before his onslaughts. Drawing Madge after him, Lambert put down his head—or believed he was doing so—and ran as fast as he could at the beings.

He bumped into some invisible forms and was slowed in his rush, but he shouted and flailed about with his arms, and tried to kick. Madge helped by screaming and striking out. They made some distance in this way, or so they thought, and the horrid creatures gave way before them.

All about them was the coppery sensation of the medium in which they moved: Lambert as he became more used to the form he was inhabiting, he began to think he could discern dreadful eyes which stared unblinkingly at the couple.

He fought on, and believed they had come to a spot where the beings did not molest them, though they still sensed the things glaring at them.

Were they on some invisible eminence, above the reach of these queer creatures?

"We might as well stop here, for if we try to go farther we may come to a worse place," said Lambert.

They rested there, in temporary peace, together at last.

"I seem to be happy now," said Madge, clinging close. "I feared I would never see you again. John dear. I ran to you when you called out that day and when I crossed the plate, I was torn and racked and knocked down. When I next experienced sensation, it was in this terrible form. I am becoming more used to it, but I kept crying out for you: the beings, as soon as they discovered my presence, began to torment me. More and more have been collecting, and I have a sensation of seeing them as horrible, revolting beasts. Oh, John, I don't think I could have stood it much longer, if you hadn't come to me. They were driving me on, on, on, ceaselessly torturing me."

"Curse them," said Lambert. "I wish I could really get hold of some of them. Perhaps, Madge, I will be able to think of some escape for us from this Hell's Dimension."

"Yes, darling. I could not bear to think that we are eternally damned to exist among these beings, hurt by them and unable to get away. How I wish we were back in the laboratory, at the tea table. How happy we were there!"

"And we will be again, Madge." Lambert was far from feeling hopeful, but he tried to encourage the girl into thinking they might get away.

However, he was unable to dissimulate. She felt his anguish for her safety. "But I know now that you love me. I can feel it stronger than ever before, John. It seems like a great rock to which I can always cling, your love. It projects me from the hatred that these beasts pour out against us."

Since they had no sense of time, they could not tell how long they were allowed to remain unmolested. But in each other's company they were happy, though each one was afraid for the safety of the loved one.

They spoke of the mortal life they had lived, and their love. They felt no need of food or water, but clung together in a dimensionless universe, held up by love.

The lull came to an end, at last. There was no change in the coppery vagueness about them which they sensed as the surrounding ether, but all was changeless, boundless. Lambert, close to Madge Crawford, felt that they were about to be attacked.

He had swift, temporary impressions of seeing saucerlike, unblinking eyes, and then hordes of bizarre inhabitants started to climb up to their perch.

For a short while, Lambert and Madge fought them off, thrusting at them, seeming to push them backward down the intangible slope; the cries which the dematerialized humans uttered also helped to hold the leaders of the attacking army partially in check, but the vast number of beings swept forward.

The thrusts of the torture-fields they emanated became more and more racking, as the two unfortunates shuddered in horror and pain.

The power to demonstrate loud noise was evidently impossible to the creatures, for their only sounds came to Madge Crawford and John Lambert as long-drawn out, almost unbearable squeaks, mouse-like in character.

Perhaps they had never had the faculty of speech, since they did not need it to communicate with one another; perhaps they realized that the racket they could make would hurt them as much as it did their enemies.

Lambert, Madge clinging to him, was forced backward down the slope, and the beings had the advantage of height. He could not again reach the eminence, but the way behind seemed to clear quickly enough, though thrusts were made at him, innumerable times with the torture-fields.

The hordes pushed them backward, and ever back.

They were forced on for some distance. As they retreated, the way become easier, and fewer and fewer of the beings impeded the channel along which they moved, though in front of them and on all sides, above, beneath, they were pressed by the hordes.

"They are forcing us to some place they want us to go," said Lambert desperately.

"We can do nothing more," replied the girl.

Lambert felt her quiet confidence in him, and that as long as they were together, all was well.

"Maybe they can kill us, somehow," he said.

And now, Lambert felt the way was clear to the rear. There was a sudden rush of the creatures, and needlelike fields were impelled viciously into the spaces the two humans occupied.

Madge cried out in pain, and Lambert shouted. The throng drew away from them as suddenly as it had surged forward, and an instant later the pair, clinging together, felt that they were falling, falling, falling....

"Are you all right, Madge?"

"Yes, John."

But he knew she was suffering. How long they fell he did not know, but they stopped at last. No sooner had they come to rest than they were assailed with sensations of pain which made both cry out in anguish.

There, in the spot where they had been thrust by the hordes, they felt that there was some terrific vibration which racked and tore at their invisible forms continuously, sending them into spasms of sharp misery.

They both were forced to give vent to their feelings by loud cries. But they could not command their movements any longer. When they tried to get away, their limbs moved but they felt that they remained in the same spot.

The pain shook every fraction of their souls.

"We—we are in some pit of hell, into which they have thrown us, John," gasped Madge.

He knew she was shivering with the torture of that great vibration from which there was no escape, that they were in a prison-pit of Hell's Dimension.

"I—oh—John—I'm dying!"

But he was powerless to help her. He suffered as much as she. Yet there was no weakening of his sensations; he was in as much torture as he had been at the start. He knew that they could not die and could never escape from this misery of hell.

Their cries seemed to disturb the vacuum about. Lambert, shivering and shaking with pain, was aware that great eyes, similar to those which they had thought they saw above, were now upon them. Squeaks were impressed upon him, squeaks which expressed disapprobation. There were some of the beings in the pit with them.

Madge knew they were there, too. She cried out in terror, "Will they add to our misery?"

But the creatures in the vacuum were pinned to the spots they occupied, as were Madge and Lambert. From their squeaks it was evident they suffered, too, and were fellow prisoners of the mortals.

"Probably the cries we make disturb them," said Lambert. "Vibrations to which we and they are not attuned are torture to the form we are in. Evidently the inhabitants of this hell world punish offenders by condemning them to this eternal torture."

"Why—why did they treat us so?"

"Perhaps we jarred upon them, hurt them, because we were not of their kind exactly," said Lambert. "Perhaps it was just their natural hatred of us as strangers."

They did not grow used to the terrible eternity of torments. No, if anything, it grew worse as it went on. Still, they could visualize no end to the existence to which they were bound. Throbs of awful intensity rent them, tore them apart myriad times, yet they still felt as keenly as before and suffered just as much. There was no death for them, no release from the intangible world in which they were.

Their fellow prisoners squeaked at them, as though imploring them not to add to the agony by uttering discordant cries. But it was impossible for Madge to keep quiet, and Lambert shouted in anguish from time to time.

There seemed to be no end to it.

And yet, after what was eternity to the sufferers, Madge spoke hopefully.

"Darling John, I—I fear I am really going to die. I am growing weaker. I can feel the pain very little now. It is all vague, and is getting less real to me. Good-by, sweetheart, I love you, and I always will—"

Lambert uttered a strangled cry, "No, no. Don't leave me, Madge."

He clung to her, yet she was becoming extremely intangible to him. She was melting away from his embrace, and Lambert felt that he, too, was weaker, even less real than he had been. He hoped that if it was the end, they would go together.

Desperately, he tried to hold her with him, but he had little ability to do so. The torture was still racking his consciousness, but was becoming more dreamlike.

There was a terrific snap, suddenly, and Lambert lost all consciousness....

"Water, water!"

Lambert, opening his eyes, felt his body writhing about, and experienced pain that was—mortal. A bluish-green light dazzled his pupils and made him blink.

Something cut into his flesh, and Lambert rolled about, trying to escape. He bumped into something, something soft; he clung to this form, and knew that he was holding on to a human being. Then the light died out, and in its stead was the yellow, normal glow of the electric lights. Weak, famished, almost dead of thirst, Lambert looked about him at the familiar sights of his laboratory. He was lying on the floor, close by the metal plate, and at his side, unconscious but still alive to judge by her rising and falling breast, was Madge Crawford.

Someone bent over him, and pressed a glass of water against his lips. He drank, watching while a mortal whom Lambert at last realized was Detective Phillips bathed Madge Crawford's temples with water from a pitcher and forced a little between her pale, drawn lips.

Lambert tried to rise, but he was weak, and required assistance. He was dazed, still, and they sat him down in a chair and allowed him to come to.

He shuddered from time to time, for he still thought he could feel the torture which he had been undergoing. But he was worried about Madge, and watched anxiously as Phillips, assisted by another man, worked over the girl.

At last, Madge stirred and moaned faintly. They lifted her to a bench, where they gently restored her to full consciousness.

When she could sit up, she at once cried out for Lambert.

The scientist had recovered enough to rise to his feet and stagger toward her. "Here I am, darling," he said.

"John—we're alive—we're back in the laboratory!"

"Ah, Lambert. Glad to see you." A heavy voice spoke, and Lambert for the first time noticed the black-clad figure which stood to one side, near the switchboard, hidden by a large piece of apparatus.

"Dr. Morgan!" cried Lambert.

Althaus Morgan, the renowned physicist, came forward calmly, with outstretched hand. "So, you realized your great ambition, eh?" he said curiously. "But where would you be if I had not been able to bring you back?"

"In Hell—or Hell's Dimension, anyway," said Lambert.

He went to Madge, took her in his arms. "Darling, we are safe. Morgan has managed to re-materialize us. We will never again be cast into the void in this way. I shall destroy the apparatus and my notes."

Doherty, who had been out of the room on some errand, came into the laboratory. He shouted when he saw Lambert standing before him.

"So you got him," he cried. "Where was he hidin'?"

His eyes fell upon Madge Crawford, then, and he exclaimed in satisfaction. "You found her, eh?"

"No," said Phillips. "They came back. They suddenly appeared out of nothing, Doherty."

"Don't kid me," growled Doherty. "They were hidin' in a closet somewhere. Maybe they can fool you guys, but not me."

Lambert spoke to Phillips. "I'm starving to death and I think Miss Crawford must be, too. Will you tell Felix to bring us some food, plenty of it?"

One of the sleuths went to the kitchen to give the order. Lambert turned to Morgan.

"How did you manage to bring us back?" he asked.

Morgan shrugged. "It was all guess work at the last. I at first could check the apparatus by your notes, and this took some time. You know you have written me in detail about what you were working on, so when I was summoned by Detective Phillips, who said you had mentioned my name to him as the only one who could help, I could make a good conjecture as to what had occurred. I heard the stories of all concerned, and realized that you must have dematerialized Miss Crawford by mistake, and then, unable to bring her back, had followed her yourself.

"I put on your insulation outfit, and went to work. I have not left here for a moment, but have snatched an hour or two of sleep from time to time. Detective Phillips has been very good and helpful.

"Finally, I had everything in shape, but I reversed the apparatus in vital spots, and tried each combination until suddenly, a few minutes ago, you were re-materialized. It was a desperate chance, but I was forced to take it in an endeavor to save you."

Lambert held out his hand to his friend. "I can never thank you enough," he said gratefully. "You saved us from a horrible fate. But you speak as though we had been gone a long while. Was it many hours?"

"Hours?" repeated Morgan, his lips parting under his black beard. "Man, it was eight days! You have been gone since a week ago last night!"

Lambert turned to Phillips. "I must ask you not to release this story to the newspapers," he begged.

Phillips smiled and turned up his hands in a gesture of frank wonder. "Professor Lambert," he said, "I can't believe what I have seen myself. If I told such a yarn to the reporters, they'd never forget it. They'd kid me out of the department."

"Aw, they were hidin' in a closet," growled Doherty. "Come on, we've wasted too much time on this job already. Just a couple of nuts, says I."

The sleuths, after Phillips had shaken hands with Lambert, left the laboratory. Morgan, a large man of middle age, joined them in a meal which Felix served to the three on a folding table brought in for the purpose. Felix was terribly glad to see Madge and Lambert again, and manifested his joy by many bobs and leaps as he waited upon them. A grin spread across his face from ear to ear.

Morgan asked innumerable questions. They described as best they could what they could recall of the strange dominion in which they had been, and the physicist listened intently.

"It is some Hell's Dimension, as you call it," he said at last.

"Where it is, or exactly what, I cannot say," said Lambert. "I surely have no desire to return to that world of hate."

Madge, happy now, smiled at him and he leaned over and kissed her tenderly.

"We have come from Hell, together," said Lambert, "and now we are in Heaven!"

IN THE NEXT ISSUE

DARK MOON

A Complete Novelette of Adventure on a Mysterious New Satellite

By Charles W. Diffin

WHEN CAVERNS YAWNED

Another of the Immensely Popular Dr. Bird Exploits

By Captain S. P. Meek

THE DEATH-CLOUD

A Thrilling Spy Story of the Great War of 1995

By Nat Schachner *and* Arthur L. Zagat

THE EXILE OF TIME

Part Two of the Epic New Novel

By Ray Cummings

—And Others!

They fell, for hours,
into a deep chasm.

THE WORLD BEHIND
THE MOON

By Paul Ernst

Like pitiless jaws, a distant crater opened for their ship. Helplessly, they hurtled toward it: helplessly, because they were still in the nothingness of space, with no atmospheric resistance on which their rudders, or stern or bow tubes, could get a purchase to steer them.

Professor Dorn Wichter waited anxiously for the slight vibration that should announce that the projectile-shaped shell had entered the new planet's atmosphere.

> Two intrepid Earth-men fight it out with the horrific monsters of Zeud's frightful jungles.

"Have we struck it yet?" asked Joyce, a tall blond young man with the shoulders of an athlete and the broad brow and square chin of one who combines dreams with action. He made his way painfully toward Wichter. It was the first time he had attempted to move since the shell had passed the neutral point—that belt midway between the moon and the world behind it, where the pull of gravity of each satellite was neutralized by the other. They, and all the loose objects in the shell, had floated uncomfortably about the middle of the chamber for half an hour or so, gradually settling down again; until now it was possible, with care, to walk.

"Have we struck it?" he repeated, leaning over the professor's shoulder and staring at the resistance gauge.

"No." Absently Wichter took off his spectacles and polished them. "There's not a trace of resistance yet."

They gazed out the bow window toward the vast disc, like a serrated, pockmarked plate of blue ice, that was the planet Zeud—discovered and named by them. The same thought was in the mind of each. Suppose there were no atmosphere surrounding Zeud to cushion their descent into the hundred-mile crater that yawned to receive them?

"Well," said Joyce after a time, "we're taking no more of a chance here than we did when we pointed our nose toward the moon. We were almost sure that was no atmosphere there—which meant we'd nose dive into the rocks at five thousand miles an hour. On Zeud there might be anything." His eyes shone. "How wonderful that there should be such a planet, unsuspected during all the centuries men have been studying the heavens!"

Wichter nodded agreement. It was indeed wonderful. But what was more wonderful was its present discovery: for that would never have transpired had not he and Joyce succeeded in their attempt to fly to the moon. From there, after following the sun in its slow journey around to the lost side of the lunar globe—that face which the earth has never yet observed—they had seen shining in the near distance the great ball which they had christened Zeud.

Astronomical calculations had soon described the mysterious hidden satellite. It was almost a twin to the moon; a very little smaller, and less than eighty thousand miles away. Its rotation was nearly similar, which made its days not quite sixteen of our earthly days. It was of approximately the weight, per cubic mile, of Earth. And there it whirled, directly in a line with the earth and the moon, moving as the moon moved so that it was ever out of sight beyond it, as a dime would be out of sight if placed in a direct line behind a penny.

Zeud, the new satellite, the world beyond the moon! In their excitement at its discovery, Joyce and Wichter had left the moon—which they had found to be as dead and cold as it had been surmised to be—and returned summarily to Earth. They had replenished their supplies and their oxygen tanks, and had come back—to circle around the moon and point the sharp prow of the shell toward Zeud. The gift of the moon to Earth was a dubious one; but the gift of a possibly living planet-colony to mankind might be the solution of the overcrowded conditions of the terrestial sphere!

"Speed, three thousand miles an hour," computed Wichter. "Distance to Zeud, nine hundred and eighty miles. If we don't strike a few atoms of hydrogen or something soon we're going to drill this nearest crater a little deeper!"

Joyce nodded grimly. At two thousand miles from Earth there had still been enough hydrogen traces in the ether to give purchase to the explosions of their water-motor. At six hundred miles from the moon they had run into a sparse gaseous belt that had enabled them to change direction and slow their speed. They had hoped to find hydrogen at a thousand or twelve hundred miles from Zeud.

"Eight hundred and thirty miles," commented Wichter, his slender, bent body tensed. "Eight hundred miles—ah!"

A thrumming sound came to their ears as the shell quivered, imperceptibly almost, but unmistakeably, at the touch of some faint resistance outside in space.

"We've struck it, Joyce. And it's much denser than the moon's, even as we'd hoped. There'll be life on Zeud, my boy, unless I'm vastly mistaken. You'd better look to the motor now."

Joyce went to the water-motor. This was a curious, but extremely simple affair. There was a glass box, ribbed with polished steel, about the size and shape of a cigar box, which was full of water. Leading away from this, to the bow and stern of the shell, were two small pipes. The pipes were greatly thickened for a period of three feet or so, directly under the little tank, and were braced by bed-plates so heavy as to look all out of proportion. Around the thickened parts of the pipes were coils of heavy, insulated copper wire. There were no valves nor cylinders, no revolving parts: that was all there was to the "motor."

Joyce didn't yet understand the device. The water dripped from the tank, drop by drop, to be abruptly disintegrated, made into an explosive, by being subjected to a powerful magnetic field induced in the coils by a generator in the bow of the shell. As each drop of water passed into the pipes, and was instantaneously broken up, there was a violent but controlled explosion— and the shell was kicked another hundred miles ahead on its journey. That was all Joyce knew about it.

He threw the bow switch. There was a soft shock as the motor exhausted through the forward tube, slowing their speed.

"Turn on the outside generator propellers," ordered Wichter. "I think our batteries are getting low."

Joyce slipped the tiny, slim-bladed propellers into gear. They began to turn, slowly at first in the almost non-existent atmosphere.

"Four hundred miles," announced Wichter. "How's the temperature?"

Joyce stepped to the thermometer that registered the heat of the outer wall. "Nine hundred degrees," he said.

"Cut down to a thousand miles an hour," commanded Wichter. "Five hundred as soon as the motor will catch that much. I'll keep our course straight toward this crater. It's in wells like that, that we'll find livable air—if we're right in believing there is such a thing on Zeud."

Joyce glanced at the thermometer. It still registered hundreds of degrees, though their speed had been materially reduced.

"I guess there's livable air, all right," he said. "It's pretty thick outside already."

The professor smiled. "Another theory vindicated. I was sure that Zeud, swinging on the outside of the Earth-moon-Zeud chain and hence traveling at a faster rate, would pick up most of the moon's atmosphere over a period of millions of years. Also it must have been shielded by the moon, to some extent, against the constant small atmospheric leakage most celestial globes are subject to. Just the same, when we land, we'll test conditions with a rat or two."

At a signal from him, Joyce checked their speed to four hundred miles an hour, then to two hundred, and then, as they descended below the highest rim of the circular cliffs of the crater, almost to a full stop. They floated toward the surface of Zeud, watching with breathless interest the panorama that unfolded beneath them.

They were nosing toward a spot that was being favored with the Zeudian sunrise. Sharp and clear the light rays slanted down, illuminating about half the crater's floor and leaving the cliff protected half in dim shadow.

The illuminated part of the giant pit was as bizarre as the landscape of a nightmare. There were purplish trees, immense beyond belief. There were broad, smooth pools of inky black fluid that was oily and troubled in spots as though disturbed by some moving things under the surface. There were bare, rocky patches where the stones, the long drippings of ancient lava flow, were spread like bleaching gray skeletons of monsters. And over all, rising from pools and bare ground and jungle alike, was a thin, miasmic mist.

Sustained by the slow, steady exhaust of the motor, rising a little with each partly muffled explosion and sinking a little further in each interval, they settled toward a bare, lava strewn spot that appealed to Wichter as being a good landing place. With a last hiss, and a grinding jar, they grounded. Joyce opened the switch to cut off the generator.

"Now let's see what the air's like," said Wichter, lifting down a small cage in which was penned an active rat.

He opened a double panel in the shell's hull, and freed the little animal. In an agony of suspense they watched it as it leaped onto the bare lava and halted a moment....

"Seems to like it," said Joyce, drawing a great breath.

The rat, as though intoxicated by its sudden freedom, raced away out of sight, covering eight or ten feet at a bound, its legs scurrying ludicrously in empty air during its short flights.

"That means that we can dispense with oxygen helmets—and that we'd better take our guns," said Wichter, his voice tense, his eyes snapping behind his glasses.

He stepped to the gun rack. In this were half a dozen air-guns. Long and of very small bore, they discharged a tiny steel shell in which was a liquid of his invention that, about a second after the heat of its forced passage through the rifle barrel, expanded instantly in gaseous form to millions of times its liquid bulk. It was the most powerful explosive yet found, but one that was beautifully safe to carry inasmuch as it could be exploded only by heat.

"Are we ready?" he said, handing a gun to Joyce. "Then—let's go!"

But for a breath or two they hesitated before opening the heavy double door in the side of the hull, savoring to the full the immensity of the moment.

The rapture of the explorer who is the first to set foot on a vast new continent was theirs, magnified a hundredfold. For they were the first to set foot on a vast new planet! An entire new world, containing heaven alone knew what forms of life, what monstrous or infinitesimal creatures, lay before them. Even the profound awe they had experienced when landing on the moon was dwarfed by the solemnity of this occasion; just as it is less soul stirring to discover an arctic continent which is perpetually cased in barren ice, than to discover a continent which is warmly fruitful and, probably, teeming with life.

Still wordless, too stirred to speak, they opened the vault-like door and stepped out—into a humid heat which was like that of their own tropical regions, but not so unendurable.

In their short stay on the moon, during which they had taken several walks in their insulated suits, they had become somewhat accustomed to the decreased weight of their bodies due to the lesser gravity, so that here, where their weight was even less, they did not make any blunders of stepping twenty feet instead of a yard.

Walking warily, glancing alertly in all directions to guard against any strange animals that might rush out to destroy them, they moved toward the nearest stretch of jungle.

The first thing that arrested their attention was the size of the trees they were approaching. They had got some idea of their hugeness from the shell, but viewed from ground level they loomed even larger. Eight hundred, a thousand feet they reared their mighty tops, with trunks hundreds of feet in circumference; living pyramids whose bases wove together to make an impenetrable ceiling over the jungle floor. The leaves were thick and bloated like cactus growths, and their color was a pronounced lavender.

"We must take back several of those leaves," said Wichter, his scientific soul filled with cold excitement.

"I wish we could take back some of this air, too." Joyce filled his lungs to capacity. "Isn't it great? Like wine! It almost counteracts the effects of the heat."

"There's more oxygen in it than in our own," surmised Wichter. "My God! What's that!"

They halted for an instant. From the depths of the lavender jungle had come an ear shattering, screaming hiss, as though some monstrous serpent were in its death agony.

They waited to hear if the noise would be repeated. It wasn't. Dubiously they started on again.

"We'd better not go in there too far," said Joyce. "If we didn't come out again it would cost Earth a new planet. No one else knows the secret of your water-motor."

"Oh, nothing living can stand against these guns of ours," replied Wichter confidently. "And that noise might not have been caused by anything living. It might have been steam escaping from some volcanic crevice."

They started cautiously down a well defined, hard packed trail through thorny lavender underbrush. As they went, Joyce blazed marks on various tree trunks marking the direction back to the shell. The tough fibres exuded a bluish liquid from the cuts that bubbled slowly like blood.

To the right and left of them were cup-shaped bushes that looked like traps; and that their looks were not deceiving was proved by a muffled, bleating cry that rose from the compressed leaves of one of them they passed. Sluggish, blind crawling things like three-foot slugs flowed across their path and among the tree trunks, leaving viscous trails of slime behind them. And there were larger things....

"Careful," said Wichter suddenly, coming to a halt and peering into the gloom at their right.

"What did you see?" whispered Joyce.

Wichter shook his head. The gigantic, two-legged, purplish figure he had dimly made out in the steamy dark, had moved away. "I don't know. It looked a little like a giant ape."

They halted and took stock of their situation, mechanically wiping perspiration from their streaming faces, and pondering as to whether or not they should turn back. Joyce, who was far from being a coward, thought they should.

"In this undergrowth," he pointed out, "we might be rushed before we could even fire our guns. And we're nearly a mile from the shell."

But Wichter was like an eager child.

"We'll press on just a little," he urged. "To that clear spot in front of us." He pointed along the trail to where sunlight was blazing down through an opening in the trees. "As soon as we see what's there, we'll go back."

With a shrug, Joyce followed the eager little man down the weird trail under the lavender trees. In a few moments they had reached the clearing which was Wichter's goal. They halted on its edge, gazing at it with awe and repulsion.

It was a circular quagmire of festering black mud about a hundred yards across. Near at hand they could see the mud heaving, very slowly, as though abysmal forms of life were tunneling along just under the surface. They glanced toward the center of the bog, which was occupied by one of the smooth black pools, and cried aloud at what they saw.

At the brink of the pool was lying a gigantic creature like a great, thick snake—a snake with a lizard's head, and a series of many-jointed, scaled legs running down its powerful length. Its mouth was gaping open to reveal hundreds of needle-sharp, backward pointing teeth. Its legs and thick, stubbed tail were threshing feebly in the mud as though it were in distress; and its eyes, so small as to be invisible in its repulsive head, were glazed and dull.

"Was that what we heard back a ways?" wondered Joyce.

"Probably," said Wichter. His eyes shone as he gazed at the nightmare shape. Impulsively he took a step toward the stirring mud.

"Don't be entirely insane," snapped Joyce, catching his arm.

"I must see it closer," said Wichter, tugging to be free.

"Then we'll climb a tree and look down on it. We'll probably be safer up off the ground anyway."

They ascended the nearest jungle giant—whose rubbery bark was so ringed and scored as to be as easy to climb as a staircase—to the first great bough, about fifty feet from the ground, and edged out till they hung over the rim of the quagmire. From there, with the aid of their binoculars, they expected to see the dying monster in every detail. But when they looked toward the pool it was not in sight!

"Were we seeing things?" exclaimed Wichter, rubbing his glasses. "I'd have sworn it was lying there!"

"It was," said Joyce grimly. "Look at the pool. That'll tell you where it went."

The black, secretive surface was bubbling and waving as though, down in its depths, a terrific fight were taking place.

"Something came up and dragged our ten-legged lizard down to its den. Then that something's brothers got onto the fact that a feast was being held, and rushed in. That pool would be no place for a before-breakfast dip!"

Wichter started to say something in reply, then gazed, hypnotized, at the opposite wall of the jungle.

From the dense screen of lavender foliage stretched a glistening, scale-armored neck, as thick as a man's body at its thinnest point, which was just behind a tremendous-jawed crocodilian head. It tapered back for a distance of at least thirty feet, to merge into a body as big as that of a terrestial whale, that was supported by four squat, ponderous legs.

Moving with surprising rapidity, the enormous thing slid into the mud and began ploughing a way, belly deep, toward the pool. Shapeless, slow-writhing forms were cast up in its wake, to quiver for a moment in the sunlight and then melt below the mud again.

One of the bloated, formless mud-crawlers was snapped up in the huge jaws with an abrupt plunge of the long neck, and the monster began to feed, hog-like, slobbering over the loathsome carcass.

Wichter shook his head, half in fanatical eagerness, half in despair. "I'd like to stay and see more," he said with a sigh, "but if that's the kind of creatures we're apt to encounter in the Zeudian jungle, we'd better be going at once—"

"Sh-h!" snapped Joyce. Then, in a barely audible whisper: "I think the thing heard your voice!"

The monster had abruptly ceased its feeding. Its head, thrust high in the air, was waving inquisitively from side to side. Suddenly it expelled the air from its vast lungs in a roaring cough—and started directly for their tree.

"Shoot!" cried Wichter, raising his gun.

———

Moving with the speed of an express train, the monster had almost got to their overhanging branch before they could pull the triggers. Both shells imbedded themselves in the enormous chest, just as the long neck reached up for them. And at once things began to happen with cataclysmic rapidity.

Almost with their impact the shells exploded. The monster stopped, with a great hole torn in its body. Then, dying on its feet, it thrust its great head up and its huge jaws crunched over the branch to which its two puny destroyers were clinging.

With all its dozens of tons of weight, it jerked in a gargantuan death agony. The tree, enormous as it was, shook with it, and the branch itself was tossed as though in a hurricane.

There was a splintering sound. Wichter and Joyce dropped their guns to cling more tightly to the bole of the drooping branch that was their only security. The guns glanced off the mountainous body—and, with a last convulsion of the mighty legs, were swept underneath!

The monster was still at last, its insensate jaws yet gripping the bough. The two men looked at each other in speechless consternation. The shell a mile off through the dreadful jungle.... Themselves, helpless without their guns....

"Well," said Joyce at last. "I guess we'd better be on our way. Waiting here, thinking it over, won't help any. Lucky there's no night, for a couple of weeks at least, to come stealing down on us."

———

He started down the great trunk, with Wichter following close behind. Walking as rapidly as they could, they hurried back along the tunneled trail toward their shell.

They hadn't covered a hundred yards when they heard a mighty crashing of underbrush behind them. Glancing back, they saw tooth-studded jaws gaping cavernously at the end of a thirty-foot neck—little, dead-looking eyes glaring at them—a hundred-foot body smashing its way over the trap-bushes and through tangles of vines and down-drooping branches.

"The mate to the thing we killed back there!" Joyce panted. "Run, for God's sake!"

Wichter needed no urging. He hadn't an ounce of fear in his spare, small body. But he had an overwhelming desire to get back to Earth and deliver his message. He was trembling as he raced after Joyce, thirty feet to a bound, ducking his head to avoid hitting the thick lavender foliage that roofed the trail.

"One of us must get through!" he panted over and over. "One of us must make it!"

It was speedily apparent that they could never outrun their pursuer. The reaching jaws were only a few yards behind them now.

"You go," called Joyce, sobbing for breath. He slowed his pace deliberately.

"No—you—" Wichter slowed too. In a frenzy, Joyce shoved him along the trail.

"I tell you—"

He got no further. In front of them, where there had appeared to be solid ground, they suddenly saw a yawning pit. Desperately, they tried to veer aside, but they were too close. Their last long birdlike leap carried them over the edge. They fell, far down, into a deep chasm, splashing into a shallow pool of water.

A few clods of earth cascaded after them as the monster above dug its great splay feet into the ground and checked its rush in time to keep from falling after them. Then the top of the pit slowly darkened as a covering of some sort slid across it. They were in a prison as profoundly quiet and utterly black as a tomb.

"Dorn," shouted Joyce. "Are you all right?"

"Yes," came a voice in the near darkness. "And you?"

"I'm still in one piece as far as I can feel." There was a splashing noise. He waded toward it and in a moment his outstretched hand touched the professor's shoulder.

"This is a fine mess," he observed shakily. "We got away from those tooth-lined jaws, all right, but I'm wondering if we're much better off than we would have been if we hadn't escaped."

"I'm wondering the same thing." Wichter's voice was strained. "Did you see the way the top of the pit closed above us? That means we're in a trap. And a most ingenious trap it is, too! The roof of it is camouflaged until it looks exactly like the rest of the trail floor. The water in here is just shallow enough to let large animals break their necks when they fall in and just deep enough to preserve small animals—like ourselves—alive. We're in the hands of some sort of reasoning, intelligent beings, Joyce!"

"In that case," said Joyce with a shudder, "we'd better do our best to get out of here!"

But this was found to be impossible. They couldn't climb up out of the pit, and nowhere could they feel any openings in the walls. Only smooth, impenetrable stone met their questing fingers.

"It looks as though we're in to stay," said Joyce finally. "At least until our Zeudian hosts, whatever kind of creatures they may be, come and take us out. What'll we do then? Sail in and die fighting? Or go peaceably along with them—assuming we aren't killed at once—on the chance that we can make a break later?"

"I'd advise the latter," answered Wichter. "There is a small animal on our own planet whose example might be a good one for us to follow. That's the 'possum." He stopped abruptly, and gripped Joyce's arm.

From the opposite side of the pit came a grating sound. A crack of greenish light appeared, low down near the water. This widened jerkily as though a door were being hoisted by some sort of pulley arrangement. The walls of the pit began to glow faintly with reflected light.

"Down," breathed Wichter.

Noiselessly they let themselves sink into the water until they were floating, eyes closed and motionless, on the surface. Playing dead to the best of their ability, they waited for what might happen next.

They heard a splashing near the open rock door. The splashing neared them, and high-pitched hissing syllables came to their ears—variegated sounds that resembled excited conversation in some unknown language.

Joyce felt himself touched by something, and it was all he could do to keep from shouting aloud and springing to his feet at the contact.

He'd had no idea, of course, what might be the nature of their captors, but he had imagined them as man-like, to some extent at least. And the touch of his hand, or flipper, or whatever it was, indicated that they were not!

They were cold-blooded, reptilian things, for the flesh that had touched him was cold; as clammy and repulsive as the belly of a dead fish. So repulsive was that flesh that, when he presently felt himself lifted high up and roughly carried, he shuddered in spite of himself at the contact.

Instantly the thing that bore him stopped. Joyce held his breath. He felt an excruciating, stabbing pain in his arm, after which the journey through the water was resumed. Stubbornly he kept up his pretence of lifelessness.

The splashing ceased, and he heard flat wet feet slapping along on dry rock, indicating that they had emerged from the pit. Then he sank into real unconsciousness.

The next thing he knew was that he was lying on smooth, bare rock in a perfect bedlam of noises. Howls and grunts, snuffling coughs and snarls beat at his ear-drums. It was as though he had fallen into a vast cage in which were hundreds of savage, excited animals—animals, however, that in spite of their excitement and ferocity were surprisingly motionless, for he heard no scraping of claws, or padding of feet.

Cautiously he opened his eyes....

He was in a large cave, the walls of which were glowing with greenish, phosphorescent light. Strewn about the floor were seemingly dead carcasses of animals. And what carcasses there were! Blubber-coated things that looked like giant tadpoles, gazelle-like creatures with a single, long slim horn growing from delicate small skulls, four-legged beasts and six-legged ones, animals with furry hides and crawlers with scaled coverings—several hundred assorted specimens of the smaller life of Zeud lay stretched out in seeming lifelessness.

But they were not dead, these bizarre beasts of another world. They lived, and were animated with the frenzied fear of trapped things. Joyce could see the tortured heaving of their furred and scaled sides as they panted with terror. And from their throats issued the outlandish noises he had heard. They were alive enough—only they seemed unable to move!

There was nothing in his range of vision that might conceivably be the beings that had captured them, so Joyce started to lift his head and look around at the rest of the cavern. He found that he could not move. He tried again, and his body was as unresponsive as a log. In fact, he couldn't feel his body at all! In growing terror, he concentrated all his will on moving his arm. It was as limp as a rag.

He relaxed, momentarily in the grip of stark, blind panic. He was as helpless as the howling things around him! He was numbed, completely paralyzed into immobility!

The professor's voice—a weak, uncertain voice—sounded from behind him. "Joyce! Joyce!"

He found that he could talk, that the paralysis that gripped the rest of his muscles had not extended to the vocal cords. "Dorn! Thank God you're alive! I couldn't see you, and I thought—"

"I'm alive, but that's about all," said Wichter. "I—I can't move."

"Neither can I. We've been drugged in some manner—just as all the other animals in here have been drugged. I must have got my dose in the pit. I was cut, or stabbed, in the arm."

Joyce stopped talking as he suddenly heard steps, like human footsteps yet weirdly different—flap-flapping sounds as though awkward flippers were slapping along the rock floor toward them. The steps stopped within a few feet of them; then, after what seemed hours, they sounded again, this time in front of him.

He opened his eyes, cautiously, barely moving his eyelids, and saw at last, in every hideous detail, one of the super-beasts that had captured Wichter and himself.

It was a horrible cartoon of a man, the thing that stood there in the greenish glow of the cave. Nine or ten feet high, it loomed; hairless, with a faintly iridescent, purplish hide. A thick, cylindrical trunk sloped into a neck only a little smaller than the body itself. Set on this was a bony, ugly head that was split clear across by lipless jaws. There was no nose, only slanted holes like the nostrils of an animal; and over these were set pale, expressionless, pupil-less eyes. The arms were short and thick and ended in bifurcated lumps of flesh like swollen hands encased in old-fashioned mittens. The legs were also grotesquely short, and the feet mere shapeless flaps.

It was standing near one of the smaller animals, apparently regarding it closely. Observing it himself, Joyce saw that it was moving a little. As though coming out of a coma, it was raising its bizarre head and trying to get on its feet.

Leisurely the two-legged monster bent over it. Two long fangs gleamed in the lipless mouth. These were buried in the neck of the reviving beast—and instantly it sank back into immobility.

Having reduced it to helplessness—the monster ate it! The lipless jaws gaped widely. The shapeless hands forced in the head of the animal. The throat muscles expanded hugely: and in less than a minute it had swallowed its living prey as a boa-constrictor swallows a monkey.

Joyce closed his eyes, feeling weak and nauseated. He didn't open them again till long after he had heard the last of the awkward, flapping footsteps.

"Could you see it?" asked Wichter, who was lying so closely behind him that he couldn't observe the monstrous Zeudian. "What did it do? What was it like?"

Joyce told him of the way the creature had fed. "We are evidently in their provision room," he concluded. "They keep some of their food alive, it seems.... Well, it's a quick death."

"Tell me more about the way the other animal moved, just before it was eaten."

"There isn't much to tell," said Joyce wearily. "It didn't move long after those fangs were sunk into it."

"But don't you see!" There was sudden hope in Wichter's voice. "That means that the effect of the poison, which is apparently injected by those fangs, wears off after a time. And in that case—"

"In that case," Joyce interjected, "we'd have only an unknown army of ten-foot Zeudians, the problem of finding a way to the surface of the ground again, and the lack of any kind of weapons, to keep us from escaping!"

"We're not quite weaponless, though," the professor whispered back. "Over in a corner there's a pile of the long, slender horns that sprout from the heads of some of these creatures. Evidently the Zeudians cut them out, or break them off before eating that particular type of animal. They'd be as good as lances, if we could get hold of them."

Joyce said nothing, but hope began to beat in his own breast. He had noticed a significant happening during the age-long hours in the commissary cave. Most of the Zeudians had entered from the direction of the pit. But one had come in through an opening in the opposite side. And this one had blinked pale eyes as though dazzled from bright sunlight—and was bearing some large, woody looking tubers that seemed to have been freshly uprooted! There was a good chance, thought Joyce, that that opening led to a tunnel up to the world above!

He drew a deep breath—and felt a dim pain in his back, caused by the cramping position in which he had lain for so long.

He could have shouted aloud with the thrill of that discovery. This was the first time he had felt his body at all! Did it mean that the effect of the poison was wearing off—that it wasn't as lastingly paralyzing to his earthly nerve centers as to those of Zeudian creatures around them? He flexed the muscles of his leg. The leg moved a fraction of an inch.

"Dorn!" he called softly, "I can move a little! Can you?"

"Yes," Wichter answered, "I've been able to wriggle my fingers for several minutes. I think I could walk in an hour or two."

"Then pray for that hour or two. It might mean our escape!" Joyce told him of the seldom used entrance that he thought led to the open air. "I'm sure it goes to the surface, Dorn. Those woody looking tubers had been freshly picked."

Three of the two-legged monsters came in just then. They relapsed into lifeless silence. There was a horrible moment as the three paused over them longer than any of the others had. Was it obvious that the effects of the numbing poison was wearing off? Would they be bitten again—or eaten?

The Zeudians finally moved on, hissing and clicking to each other. Eventually the cold-blooded things fed, and dragged lethargically out of the cave in the direction of the pit.

With every passing minute Joyce could feel life pouring back into his numbed body. His cramped muscles were in agony now—a pain that gave him fierce pleasure. At last, risking observation, he lifted his head and then struggled to a sitting position and looked around.

No Zeudian was in sight. Evidently they were too sure of their poison glands to post a guard over them. He listened intently, and could hear no dragging footsteps. He turned to Wichter, who had followed his example and was sitting up, feebly rubbing his body to restore circulation.

"Now's our chance," he whispered. "Stand up and walk a little to steady your legs, while I go over and get us a couple of those sharp horns. Then we'll see where that entrance of mine goes!"

He walked to the pile of bones and horns in the corner and selected two of the longest and slimmest of the ivory-like things. Just as he had rejoined Wichter he heard the sound with which he was now so grimly familiar— flapping, awkward footsteps. Wildly he signaled the professor. They dropped in their tracks, just as the approaching monster stumped into the cave.

―――――――――――

For an instant he dared hope that their movement had gone unobserved, but his hope was rudely shattered. He heard a sharp hiss: heard the Zeudian flap toward them at double-quick time. Abandoning all pretense, he sprang to his feet just as the thing reached him, its fangs gleaming wickedly in the greenish light.

He leaped to the side, going twenty feet or more with the press of his Earth muscles against the reduced gravity. The creature rushed on toward the professor. That game little man crouched and awaited its onslaught. But Joyce had sprung back again before the two could clash.

He raised the long horn and plunged it into the smooth, purplish back. Again and again he drove it home, as the monster writhed under him. It had enormous vitality. Gashed and dripping, it yet struggled on, attempting to encircle Joyce with its stubby arms. Once it succeeded, and he felt his ribs crack as it contracted its powerful body. But a final stroke finished the savage fight. He got up and, with an incoherent cry to Wichter, raced toward the opening on which they pinned their hopes of reaching the upper air.

Hissing cries and the thudding of many feet came to them just as they reached the arched mouth of the passage. But the cries, and the constant pandemonium of the paralysed animals died behind them as they bounded along the tunnel.

They emerged at last into the sunlight they had never expected to see again, beside one of the great lavender trees. They paused an instant to try to get their bearings.

"This way," panted Joyce as he saw, on a hard-packed path ahead of them, one of the trail-marks he had blazed.

Down the trail they raced, toward their space shell. Fortunately they met none of the tremendous animals that infested the jungles; and their journey to the clearing in which the shell was lying was accomplished without accident.

"We're safe now," gasped Wichter, as they came in sight of the bare lava patch. "We can outrun them five feet to their one!"

They burst into the clearing—and halted abruptly. Surrounding the shell, stumping curiously about it and touching it with their shapeless hands, were dozens of the Zeudians.

"My God!" groaned Joyce. "There must be at least a hundred of them! We're lost for certain now!"

They stared with hopeless longing at the vehicle that, if only they could reach it, could carry them back to Earth. Then they turned to each other and clasped hands, without a word. The same thought was in the mind of each— to rush at the swarming monsters and fight till they were killed. There was absolutely no chance of winning through to the shell, but it was infinitely better to die fighting than be swallowed alive.

So engrossed were the Zeudians by the strange thing that had fallen into their province, that Joyce and Wichter got within a hundred feet of them before they turned their pale eyes in their direction. Then, baring their fangs, they streamed toward the Earth men, just as the pursuing Zeudians entered the clearing from the jungle trail.

The two prepared to die as effectively as possible. Each grasped his lace-like horn tightly. The professor mechanically adjusted his glasses more firmly on his nose....

With his move, the narrowing circle of Zeudians halted. A violent clamor broke out among them. They glared at the two, but made no further step toward them.

"What in the world—" began Wichter bewilderedly.

"Your glasses!" Joyce shouted, gripping his shoulder. "When you moved them, they all stopped! They must be afraid of them, somehow. Take them clear off and see what happens."

Wichter removed his spectacles, and swung them in his hand, peering near-sightedly at the crowding Zeudians.

Their reaction to his simple move was remarkable! Hisses of consternation came from their lipless mouths. They faced each other uneasily, waving their stubby arms and covering their own eyes as though suddenly afraid they would lose them.

Taking advantage of their indecision, Joyce and Wichter walked boldly toward them. They moved aside, forming a reluctant lane. Some of the Zeudians in the rear shoved to close in on them, but the ones in front held them back. It wasn't until the two were nearly through that the lane began to straggle into a threatening circle around them again. The Zeudians were evidently becoming reassured by the fact that Wichter continued to see all right in spite of the little strange creature's alarming act of removing his eyes.

"Do it again," breathed Joyce, perspiration beading his forehead as the giants moved closed, their fangs tentatively bared for the numbing poison stroke.

Wichter popped his glasses on, then jerked them off with a cry, as though he were suffering intensely. Once more the Zeudians faltered and drew back, feeling at their own eyes.

"Run!" cried Joyce. And they raced for the haven of the shell.

The Zeudians swarmed after them, snarling and hissing. Barely ahead of the nearest, Joyce and Wichter dove into the open panel. They slammed it closed just as a powerful, stubby arm reached after them. There was a screaming hiss, and a cold, cartilagenous lump of flesh dropped to the floor of the shell—half the monster's hand, sheared off between the sharp edge of the door and the metal hull.

Joyce threw in the generator switch. With a soft roar the water-motor exploded into action, sending the shell far into the sky.

"When we return," said Joyce, adding a final thousand miles an hour to their speed before they should fly free of the atmosphere of Zeud, "I think we'd better come at the head of an army, equipped with air-guns and explosive bombs."

"And with glasses," added the professor, taking off his spectacles and gazing at them as though seeing them for the first time.

The man hurled the empty gun at the monster.

FOUR MILES WITHIN

A COMPLETE NOVELETTE

By Anthony Gilmore

CHAPTER I

The Monster of Metal

> Far down into the earth goes a gleaming metal sphere whose passengers are deadly enemies.

A strange spherical monster stood in the moonlight on the silent Mojave Desert. In the ghostly gray of the sand and sage and joshua trees its metal hide glimmered dully—an amazing object to be found on that lonely spot. But there was only pride and anticipation in the eyes of the three people who stood a little way off, looking at it. For they had constructed the strange sphere, and were soon going to entrust their lives to it.

"Professor," said one of them, a young man with a cheerful face and a likable grin, "let's go down now! There's no use waiting till to-morrow. It's always dark down there, whether it's day or night up here. Everything is ready."

The white-haired Professor David Guinness smiled tolerantly at the speaker, his partner, Phil Holmes. "I'm kind of eager to be off, myself," he admitted. He turned to the third person in the little group, a dark-haired girl. "What do you say, Sue?"

"Oh, let's, Father!" came the quick reply. "We'd never be able to sleep to-night, anyway. As Phil says, everything is ready."

"Well, I guess that settles it," Professor Guinness said to the eager young man.

Phil Holmes' face went aglow with anticipation. "Good!" he cried. "Good! I'll skip over and get some water. It's barely possible that it'll be hot down there, in spite of your eloquent logic to the contrary!" And with the words he caught up a large jug standing nearby, waved his hand, said: "I'll be right back!" and set out for the water-hole, situated nearly a mile away from their little camp. The heavy hush of the desert night settled down once more after he left.

As his figure merged with the shadows in the distance, the elderly scientist murmured aloud to his daughter:

"You know, it's good to realize that my dream is about to become a reality. If it hadn't been for Phil.... Or no—I really ought to thank you, Sue. You're the one responsible for his participation!" And he smiled fondly at the slender girl by his side.

"Phil joined us just for the scientific interest, and for the thrill of going four miles down into the earth," she retorted at once, in spite of the blush her father saw on her face. But he did not insist. Once more he turned, as to a magnet, to the machine that was his handiwork.

The fifteen-foot sphere was an earth-borer—Guinness's own invention. In it he had utilized for the first time for boring purposes the newly developed atomic disintegrators. Many holes equally spaced over the sphere were the outlets for the dissolving ray—most of them on the bottom and alternating with them on the bottom and sides were the outlets of powerful rocket propulsion tubes, which would enable it to rise easily from the hole it would presently blast into the earth. A small, tight-fitting door gave entrance to the double-walled interior, where, in spite of the space taken up by batteries and mechanisms and an enclosed gyroscope for keeping the borer on an even keel, there was room for several people.

The earth-borer had been designed not so much for scientific investigation as the specific purpose of reaching a rich store of radium ore buried four miles below the Guinness desert camp. Many geologists and mining engineers knew that the radium was there, for their instruments had proven it often; but no one up to then knew how to get to it. David Guinness did—first. The borer had been constructed in his laboratory in San Francisco, then dismantled and freighted to the little desert town of Palmdale, from whence Holmes had brought the parts to their isolated camp by truck. Strict secrecy had been kept. Rather than risk assistants they had done all the work themselves.

Fifteen minutes passed by, while the slight figure of the inventor puttered about the interior of the sphere, brightly lit by a detachable searchlight, inspecting all mechanisms in preparation for their descent. Sue stood by the door watching him, now and then turning to scan the desert for the returning Phil.

It was then, startlingly sudden, that there cracked through the velvet night the faint, distant sound of a gun. And it came from the direction of the water-hole.

Sue's face went white, and she trembled. Without a word her father stepped out of the borer and looked at her.

"That was a gun!" he said. "Phil didn't have one with him, did he?"

"No," Sue whispered. "And—why, there's nobody within miles of here!"

The two looked at each other with alarm and wonder. Then, from one of the broken patches of scrub that ringed the space in which the borer stood, came a mocking voice.

"Ah, you're mistaken, Sue," it affirmed. "But that was a gun."

David Guinness jerked around, as did his daughter. The man who had spoken stood only ten yards away, clearly outlined in the bright moonlight— a tall, well-built man, standing quite at ease, surveying them pleasantly. His smile did not change when old Guinness cried:

"Quade! James Quade!"

The man nodded and came slowly forward. He might have been considered handsome, had it not been for his thin, mocking lips and a swarthy complexion.

"What are you doing here?" demanded Guinness angrily. "And what do you mean—'it was a gun?' Have you—"

"Easy, easy—one thing at a time," said Quade, still smiling. "About the gun—well, your young friend Holmes said, he'd be right back, but I—I'm afraid he won't be."

Sue Guinness's lips formed a frightened word:

"Why?"

Quade made a short movement with his left hand, as is brushing the query aside. "Let's talk about something more pleasant," he said, and looked back at the professor. "The radium, and your borer, for instance. I hear you're all ready to go down."

David Guinness gasped. "How did you know—?" he began, but a surge of anger choked him, and his fists clenched. He stepped forward. But something came to life in James Quade's right hand and pointed menacingly at him. It was the stubby black shape of an automatic.

"Keep back, you old fool!" Quade said harshly. "I don't want to have to shoot you!"

Unwillingly, Guinness came to a stop. "What have you done with young Holmes?" he demanded.

"Never mind about him now," said Quade, smiling again. "Perhaps I'll explain later. At the moment there's something much more interesting to do. Possibly you'll be surprised to hear it, but we're all going to take a little ride in this machine of yours, Professor. Down. About four miles. I'll have to ask you to do the driving. You will, won't you—without making a fuss?"

Guinness's face worked furiously. "Why, you're crazy, Quade!" he sputtered. "I certainly won't!"

"No?" asked Quade softly. The automatic he held veered around, till it was pointing directly at the girl. "I wouldn't want to have to shoot Sue—say— through the hand...." His finger tightened perceptibly on the trigger.

"You're mad, man!" Guinness burst out. "You're crazy! What's the idea—"

"In due time I'll tell you. But now I'll ask you just once more," Quade persisted. "Will you enter that borer, or must I—" He broke off with an expressive shrug.

David Guinness was powerless. He had not the slightest idea what Quade might be about; the one thought that broke through his fear and anger was that the man was mad, and had better be humored. He trembled, and a tight sensation came to his throat at sight of the steady gun trained on his daughter. He dared not trifle.

"I'll do it," he said.

James Quade laughed. "That's better. You always were essentially reasonable, though somewhat impulsive for a man of your age. The rash way you severed our partnership, for instance.... But enough of that. I think we'd better leave immediately. Into the sphere, please. You first, Miss Guinness."

"Must she come?"

"I'm afraid so. I can't very well leave her here all unprotected, can I?"

Quade's voice was soft and suave, but an undercurrent of sarcasm ran through it. Guinness winced under it; his whole body was trembling with suppressed rage and indignation. As he stepped to the door of the earth-borer he turned and asked:

"How did you know our plans? About the radium?—the borer?"

Quade told him. "Have you forgotten," he said, "that you talked the matter over with me before we split last year? I simply had the laboratory watched, and when you got new financial backing from young Holmes, and came here. I followed you. Simple, eh?... Well, enough of this. Get inside. You first, Sue."

Trembling, the girl obeyed, and when her father hesitated Quade jammed his gun viciously into his ribs and pushed him to the door. "Inside!" he hissed, and reluctantly, hatred in his eyes, the professor stepped into the control compartment after Sue. Quade gave a last quick glance around and, with gun ever wary, passed inside. The door slammed shut: there was a click as its lock shot over. The sphere was a sealed ball of metal.

Inside, David Guinness obeyed the automatic's imperious gesture and pulled a shiny-handled lever slowly back, and the hush that rested over the Mojave was shattered by a tremendous bellow, a roar that shook the very earth. It was the disintegrating blast, hurled out of the bottom in many fan-shaped rays. The coarse gray sand beneath the machine stirred and flew wildly; the sphere vibrated madly; and then the thunder lowered in tone to a mighty humming and the earth-borer began to drop. Slowly it fell, at first, then more rapidly. The shiny top came level with the ground: disappeared; and in a moment there was nothing left but a gaping hole where a short while before a round monster of metal had stood. The hole was hot and dark, and from it came a steadily diminishing thunder....

For a long time no one in the earth-borer spoke—didn't even try to—for though the thunder of the disintegrators was muted, inside, to a steady drone, conversation was almost impossible. The three were crowded quite close in the spherical inner control compartment. Sue sat on a little collapsible stool by the bowed, but by no means subdued, figure of Professor David Guinness, while Quade sat on the wire guard of the gyroscope, which was in the exact center of the floor.

The depth gauge showed two hundred feet. Already the three people were numb from the vibration; they hardly felt any sensation at all, save one of great weight pressing inwards. The compartment was fairly cool and the air good—kept so by the automatic air rectifiers and the insulation, which shut out the heat born of their passage.

Quade had been carefully watching Guinness's manipulation of the controls, when he was struck by a thought. At once he stood up, and shouted in the elderly inventor's ear: "Try the rockets! I want to be sure this thing will go back up!"

Without a word Guinness shoved back the lever controlling the disintegrators, at the same time whirling a small wheel full over. The thudding drone died away to a whisper, and was replaced by sharper thundering, as the stream of the propulsion rockets beneath the sphere was released. A delicate needle trembled on a gauge, danced at the figure two hundred, then crept back to one-ninety ... one-sixty ... one-forty.... Quade's eyes took in everything.

"Excellent, Guinness!" he yelled. "Now—down once more!"

The rockets were slowly cut; the borer jarred at the bottom of its hole; again the disintegrators droned out. The sphere dug rapidly into the warm ground, biting lower and lower. At ten miles an hour it blasted a path to depths hitherto unattainable to man, sweeping away rock and gravel and sand— everything that stood in its way. The depth gauge rose to two thousand, then steadily to three and four. So it went on for nearly half an hour.

At the end of that time, at a depth of nearly four miles, Quade got stiffly to his feet and once more shouted into the professor's ear.

"We ought to be close to that radium, now," he said. "I think—"

But his words stopped short. The floor of the sphere suddenly fell away from their feet, and they felt themselves tumbled into a wild plunge. The drone of the disintegrators, hitherto muffled by the earth they bit into, rose to a hollow scream. Before the professor quite knew what was happening, there was a stunning crash, a shriek of tortured metal—and the earth-borer rocked and lay still....

The whole world seemed to be filled with thunder when David Guinness came back to consciousness. He opened his eyes and stared up into a darkness to which it took him some time to accustom himself. When he did, he made out hazily that he was lying on the floor of a vast dark cavern. He could dimly see its jagged roof, perhaps fifty feet above. There was the strong smell of damp earth in his nostrils; his head was splitting from the steady drone in his ear-drums. Suddenly he remembered what had happened. He groaned slightly and tried to sit up.

But he could not. His arms and legs were tied. Someone had removed him from the earth-borer and bound him on the floor of the cavern they had plunged into.

David Guinness strained at the rope. It was futile, but in doing so he twisted his head around and saw another form, similarly tied, lying close to him. He gave a little cry of relief. It was Sue. And she was conscious, her eyes on his face.

She spoke to him, but he could not understand her for the drone in his ears, and when he spoke to her it was the same. But the professor did not just then continue his effort to converse with her. His attention was drawn to the borer, now dimly illuminated by its portable light, which had been secured to the door. It was right side up, and appeared to be undamaged. The broad ray of the searchlight fell far away on one of the cavern's rough walls. He could just make out James Quade standing there, his back towards them.

He was hacking at the wall with a pick. Presently he dropped the tool and wrenched at the rock with bare hands. A large chunk came loose. He hugged it to him and turned and strode back towards the two on the floor, and as he drew near they could plainly see a gleam of triumph in his eyes.

"You know what this is?" he shouted. Guinness could only faintly hear him. "Wealth! Millions! Of course we always knew the radium was here, but this is the proof. And now we've a way of getting it out—thanks to your borer! All the credit is yours, Professor Guinness! You shall have the credit, and I'll have the money."

Guinness tugged furiously at his bonds again. "You—you—" he gasped. "How dare you tie us this way! Release us at once! What do you mean by it?"

Quade smiled unpleasantly. "You're very stupid, Guinness. Haven't you guessed by now what I'm going to do?" He paused, as if waiting for an answer, and the smile on his face gave way to a look of savage menace. For the first time his bitter feelings came to the surface.

"Have you forgotten how close I came to going to jail over those charges of yours a year ago?" he said. "Have you forgotten the disgrace to me that followed?—the stigma that forced me to disappear for months? You fool, do you think I've forgotten?—or that I'd let you—"

"Quade," interrupted the older man, "you know very well you were guilty. I caught you red-handed. You didn't fool anyone—except the jury that let you go. So save your breath, and, if you've the sense you were born with, release my daughter and me. Why, you're crazy!" he cried with mounting anger. "You can't get away with this! I'll have you in jail within forty-eight hours, once I get back to the surface!"

With an effort Quade controlled his feelings and assumed his oily, sarcastic manner. "That's just it," he said: "'once you get back!' How stupid you are! You don't seem to realize that you're not going back to the surface. You and your daughter."

Sue gasped, and her father's eyes went wide. There was a tense silence.

"You wouldn't dare!" the inventor cried finally. "You wouldn't dare!"

"It's rather large, this cavern," Quade went on. "You'll have plenty of room. Perhaps I'll untie you before I go back up, so—"

"You can't get away with it!" shouted the old man, tremendously excited. "Why, you can't, possibly! Philip Holmes'll track you down—he'll tell the police—he'll rescue us! And then—"

Quade smiled suavely. "Oh, no, he won't. Perhaps you remember the shot that sounded from the water-hole? Well, when I and my assistant, Juan, heard Holmes say he was going for water, I told Juan to follow him to the water-hole and bind him, to keep him from interfering till I got back up. But Mr. Holmes is evidently of an impulsive disposition, and must have caused trouble. Juan, too, is impulsive; he is a Mexican. And he had a gun. I'm afraid he was forced to use it.... I am quite sure Philip Holmes will not, as you say, track me down."

David Guinness looked at his daughter's white face and horror-filled eyes and suddenly crumpled. Humbly, passionately, he begged Quade to take her back up. "Why, she's never done anything to you, Quade!" he pleaded. "You can't take her life like that! Please! Leave me, if you must, but not her! You can't—"

But suddenly the old man noticed that Quade was not listening. His head was tilted to one side as if he was straining to hear something else. Guinness was held silent for a moment by the puzzled look on the other's face and the strange way he was acting.

"Do you hear it?" Quade asked at last; and without waiting for an answer, he knelt down and put his ear to the ground. When he rose his face was savage, and he cursed under his breath.

"Why, it's a humming!" muttered Professor Guinness. "And it's getting louder!"

"It sounds like another borer!" ventured Sue.

The humming grew in volume. Then, from the ceiling, a rock dropped. They were looking at the cavern roof and saw it start, but they did not hear it strike, for the ever-growing humming echoed loudly through the cavern. They saw another rock fall; and another.

"For God's sake, what is it?" cried Guinness.

Quade looked at him and slowly drew out his automatic.

"Another earth-borer, I think," he answered. "And I rather expect it contains your young friend Mr. Holmes. Yes—coming to rescue you."

For a moment Guinness and his daughter were too astounded to do anything but gape. She finally exclaimed:

"But—but then Phil's alive?"

James Quade smiled. "Probably—for the moment. But don't let your hopes rise too high. The borer he's in isn't strong enough to survive a fifty-foot plunge." He was shouting now, so loud was the thunder from above. "And," he added, "I'm afraid he's not strong enough to survive it, either!"

CHAPTER II

The Man-Hunt

When Phil Holmes started off to the water-hole, his head was full of the earth-borer and the imminent descent. Now that the long-awaited time had come, he was at fever-pitch to be off, and it did not take him long to cover the mile of sandy waste. His thoughts were far inside the earth as he dipped the jug into the clear cool water and sloshed it full.

So the rope that snaked softly through the air and dropped in a loop over his shoulders came as a stark surprise. Before he knew what was happening it had slithered down over his arms and drawn taut just above the elbows, and he was yanked powerfully backwards and almost fell.

But he managed to keep his feet as he staggered backward, and turning his head he saw the small dark figure of his aggressor some fifteen feet away, keeping tight the slack.

Phil's surprise turned to sudden fury and he completely lost his head. What he did was rash; mad; and yet, as it turned out, it was the only thing that could have saved him. Instinctively, without hesitating one second, and absolutely ignoring an excited command to stand still, he squirmed face-on to his aggressor, lowered his head and charged.

The distance was short. Halfway across it, a gun barked, and he heard the bullet crack into the water jug, which he was still holding in front of himself. And even before the splintered fragments reached the ground he had crashed into the firer.

He hit him with all the force of a tackling lineman, and they both went down. The man grunted as the wind was jarred out of him, but he wriggled like an eel and managed to worm aside and bring up his gun.

Then there was a desperate flurry of bodies in the coarse sand. Holmes dived frantically for the gun hand and caught it; but, handicapped as he was by the rope, he could not hold it. Slowly its muzzle bent upward to firing position.

Desperately, he wrenched the arm upwards, in the direction it had been straining to go, and the sudden unexpected jerk doubled the man's arm and brought the weapon across his chest. For a moment there was a test of strength as Phil lay chest to chest over his opponent, the gun blocked between. Then the other grunted; squirmed violently—and there was a muffled explosion.

A cry of pain cut the midnight air, and with insane strength Holmes' ambusher fought free from his grip, staggered to his feet and went reeling away. Phil tore loose from the rope and bounded after him, never feeling, at the moment, his powder-burned chest.

And then he halted in his tracks.

A great roar came thundering over the desert!

At once he knew that it came from the earth-borer's disintegrators. The sphere had started down without him.

He stood stock still, petrified with surprise, facing the sound, while his attacker melted farther and farther into the night. And then, suddenly, Phil Holmes was sprinting desperately back towards the Guinness camp.

He ran until he was exhausted; walked for a little while his legs gathered more strength, and his laboring lungs more air; and then ran again. As the minutes passed, the thunder lessened rapidly into a muffled drone; and by the time Phil had panted up to the brink of the hole that gaped where but a little time before the sphere was standing, it had become but a distant purr. He leaned far over and peered into the hot blackness below, but could see nothing.

Phil knelt there silently for some minutes, shocked by his strange attack, bewildered by the unexpected descent of the borer. For a time his mind would not work; he had no idea what to do. But gradually his thoughts came to order and made certain things clear.

He had been deliberately ambushed. Only by luck had he escaped, he told himself. If it hadn't been for the water jug, he'd now be out of the picture. And on the heels of the ambush had came the surprising descent of the earth-borer. The two incidents coincided too well: the same mind had planned them. And two, men, at least, were in on the plot.... It suddenly became very clear to him that the answer to the puzzle lay with the man who had ambushed him. He would have to get that man. Track him down.

Phil acted with decision. He got to his feet and strode rapidly to the deserted Guinness shack, horribly quiet and lonely now in the bright moonlight. In a minute he emerged with a flashlight at his belt and a rifle across his arm.

Once again he went over to the new black hole in the desert and looked down. From far below still came the purr, now fainter than ever. His friend, the girl he loved, were down there, he reflected bitterly, and he was helpless to reach them. Well, there was one thing he could do—go man-hunting. Turning, he started off at a long lope for the water-hole.

Ten minutes later he was there, and off to the side he found the marks of their scuffle—and small black blotches that could be nothing but blood. The other was wounded: could probably not get far. But he might still have his gun, so Phil kept his rifle handy, and tempered his impatience with caution as he set out on the trail of the widely spaced footprints.

They led off towards the nearby hills, and in the bright moonlight Phil did not use his flashlight at all, except to investigate other round black blotches that made a line parallel to the prints. As he went on he found his quarry's steps coming more closely together: becoming erratic. Soon they showed as painful drags in the sand, a laborious hauling of one foot after the other.... Phil put away his light and advanced very cautiously.

He wondered, as he went, who in the devil was behind it all. The radium-finding project had been kept strictly secret. Not another soul was supposed to know of the earth-borer and its daring mission into the heart of the earth. Yet, obviously, someone had found out, and whoever it was had laid at least part of his scheme cunningly. An old man and a girl cannot offer much resistance: he, Phil, would have been well taken care of had it not been for the water jug. So far, there were at least two in the plot: the man who had ambushed him and the unknown who had evidently kidnapped both Professor and Sue Guinness. But there might be still more.

There might be friends, nearby, of the man he was tracking. The fellow might have reached them, and warned them that the scheme hadn't gone through, that Phil was loose. They could very easily conceal themselves alongside their partner's tracks and train their rifles on the tracker....

The trail was leading up into one of the cañons in the cluster of hills to the west. For some distance he followed it up through a slash of black below the steep moonlit heights of the hills to each side—and then, suddenly, he vaguely made out the forms of two huts just ahead.

Immediately he stooped low, and went skirting widely off up one side. He proceeded slowly, with great caution, his rifle at the ready. At any moment, he knew, the hush might be split by the cracks of waylaying guns. Warily he advanced along the narrow cañon wall above the huts. No lights were lit, and the place seemed unoccupied. He was debating what to do next when his attention was attracted to a large dark object lying in the cañon trail some twenty yards from the nearest hut. Straining his eyes in the inadequate moonlight, he saw that it was the outstretched figure of a man. His quarry— his ambusher!

Phil dropped flat, fearful of being seen. Keeping as best he could in the shadows, fearing every moment to hear the sharp bark of a gun, he crawled forward. It took him a long time to approach the sprawled figure, but he wasn't taking chances. When within twenty feet, he rose suddenly and darted forward to the man's side.

His rapid glance showed him that the fellow was completely out: and another quick look around failed to show that anyone else was watching, so he returned to his examination of the man. It was the ambusher, all right: a Mexican. He was still breathing, though his face was drawn and white from the loss of blood from a wound under the blood-soaked clothing near his upper right arm. A hasty search showed that he no longer had his gun, so Phil, satisfied that he was powerless for some time to come, cautiously wormed his way towards the two shacks.

There was something sinister in the strange silence that hung over them. One was of queer construction—a windowless, square, high box of galvanized iron. The other was obviously a dwelling place. Carefully Phil sneaked up to the latter. Then, rifle ready, he pushed its door open and sent a beam of light stabbing through the darkness of the interior.

There was no one there. Only two bunks, a table, chair, a pail of water and some cooking utensils met his view. He crept out toward the other building.

Come close, Phil found that a dun-colored canvas had been thrown over the top of it, making an adequate camouflage in daytime. The place was about twenty feet high. He prowled around the metal walls and discovered a rickety door. Again, gun ready, he flung it open. The beam from his flash speared a path through the blackness—and he gasped at sight of what stood revealed.

There, inside, was a long, bullet-like tube of metal, the pointed end upper-most, and the bottom, which was flat, toward the ground. It was held in a wooden cradle, and was slanted at the floor. In the bottom were holes of two shapes—rocket tubes and disintegrating projectors. It was another earth-borer.

Phil stood frozen with surprise before this totally unlooked-for machine. He could easily have been overcome, had the owner been in the building, for he had forgotten everything but what his eyes were staring at. He started slowly around the borer, found a long narrow door slightly ajar, and stepped inside.

This borer, like Guinness's, had a double shell, and much the same instruments, though the whole job was simpler and cruder. A small instrument board contained inclination, temperature, depth and air-purity indicators, and narrow tubes led to the air rectifiers. But what kept Holmes' attention were the wires running from the magneto to the mixing chambers of the disintegrating tubes.

"The fools!" he exclaimed, "—they didn't know how to wire the thing! Or else," he added after a moment, "didn't get around to doing it." He noticed that the projectile's interior contained no gyroscope: though, he thought, none would be needed, for the machine, being long and narrow, could not change keel while in the ground. Here he was reminded of something. Stepping outside, he estimated the angle the borer made with the dirt floor. Twenty degrees. "And pointed southwest!" he exclaimed aloud. "This borer would come close to meeting the professor's, four miles under our camp!"

At once he knew what he would do. First he went back to the other shack and got the pail of water he had noticed, and took this out where the Mexican lay outstretched. He bathed the man's face and the still slightly bleeding bullet wound in his shoulder.

Presently the wounded man came to. His eyes opened, and he stared up into a steel mask of a face, in which two level black eyes bored into his. He remembered that face—remembered it all too well. He trembled, cowered away.

"No!" he gasped, as if he had seen a ghost. "No—no!"

"Yes, I'm the man," Holmes told him firmly, menacingly. "The same one you tried to ambush." He paused a moment, then said: "Do you want to live?"

It was a simple question, frightening in its simplicity.

"Because if you don't answer my questions, I'm going to let you lie here," Phil went on coldly. "And that would probably mean your death. If you do answer, I'll fix you up so you can have a chance."

The Mexican nodded eagerly. "I talk," he said.

"Good," said Phil. "Then tell me who built that machine?"

"Señor Quade. Señor James Quade."

"Quade!" Phil had heard the name before. "Of course!" he said. "Guinness's old partner!"

"I not know," the Mexican answered. "He hire me with much money. He buy thees machine inside, and we put him together. But he could no make him work—it take too long. We watch, hear old man go down to-night, and—"

The greaser stopped. "And so he sent you to get me, while he kidnapped the old man and his daughter and forced them under the ground in their own borer," Holmes supplied, and the other nodded.

"But I only mean to tie you!" he blurted, gesturing weakly. "I no mean shoot! No, no—"

"All right—forget it," Phil interrupted. "And now tell me what Quade expects to do down there."

"I not know, Señor," came the hesitant reply, "but...."

"But what?" the young man jerked.

Reluctantly the wounded Mexican continued. "Señor Quade—he—I think he don' like thees old man. I think he leave heem an' the girl down below. Then he come up an' say they keeled going down."

Phil nodded grimly. "I see," he said, voicing his thoughts. "Then he would say that he and Professor Guinness are still partners—and the radium ore will belong to him. Very nice. Very nice...."

He snapped back to action, and without another word hoisted the Mexican onto his back and carried him into the shack. There he cleansed the wound, rigged up a tight bandage for it, and tied the man to one of the cots. He tied him in such a fashion that he could reach some food and water he put by the cot.

"You leave me like thees?" the Mexican asked.

"Yes," Phil said, and started for the door.

"But what you going to do?"

Phil smiled grimly as he flung an answer back over his shoulder.

"Me?—I'm going to fix the wiring on those disintegrators in your friend Quade's borer. Then I'm starting down after him." He stopped and turned before he closed the door. "And if I don't get back—well, it's just too bad for you!"

And so, a little later, once more the hushed desert night was cleft by a furious bellow of sound. It came, this time, from a narrow cañon. The steep sides threw the roar back and back again, and the echoes swelled to an earth-shaking blast of sound. The oblong hut from which it came rocked and almost fell; then, as the noise began to lessen, teetered on its foundations and half-slipped into the ragged hole that had been bored inside.

The descent was a nightmare that Holmes would never forget. Quade's machine was much cruder and less efficient than the sphere David Guinness had designed. Its protecting insulation proved quite inadequate, and the heat rapidly grew terrific as the borer dug down. Phil became faint, stifled, and his body oozed streams of sweat. And the descent was also bumpy and uneven; often he was forced to leave the controls and work on the mechanism of the disintegrators when they faltered and threatened to stop. But in spite of everything the needle on the depth gauge gradually swung over to three thousand, and four, and five....

After the first mile Holmes improvised a way to change the air more rapidly, and it grew a little cooler. He watched the story the depth gauge told with narrowed eyes, and, as it reached three miles, inspected his rifle. At three and a half miles he stopped the borer, thinking to try to hear the noise made by the other, but so paralyzed were his ear-drums from the terrific thunder beneath, it seemed hardly any quieter when it ceased.

His plans were vague; they would have to be made according to the conditions he found. There was a coil of rope in the tube-like interior of the borer, and he hoped to find a cavern or cleft in the earth for lateral exploring. He would stop at a depth of four miles—where he should be very near the path of the professor's sphere.

But Phil never saw the needle on the gauge rise to four miles. At three and three quarters came sudden catastrophe.

He knew only that there was an awful moment of utter helplessness, when the borer swooped wildly downwards, and the floor was snatched sickeningly from under him. He was thrown violently against the instrument panel; then up toward the pointed top; and at the same instant came a rending crash that drove his senses from him....

CHAPTER III

"You Haven't the Guts"

"Fust as I thought," said James Quade in the silence that fell when the last echoes had died away, and the splinters of steel and rock had settled. "You see, Professor, this earth-borer belongs to me. Yes, I built one too. But I couldn't, unfortunately, get it working properly—that is, in time to get down here first. After all, I'm not a scientist, and remembered little enough of your borer's plans.... It's probably young Holmes who's dropped in on us. Shall we see?"

David Guinness and his daughter were speechless with dread. Quade had trained the searchlight on the borer, and by turning their heads they could see it plainly. It was all too clear that the machine was a total wreck. It had pitched over onto one side, its shell cracked and mangled irreparably. Grotesque pieces of crumpled metal lay all around it. Its slanting course had tumbled it within fifteen yards of the sphere.

In silence the old man and the girl watched Quade walk deliberately over to it, his automatic steady in his right hand. He wrenched at the long, narrow door, but it was so badly bent that for a while he could not get it open. At last it swung out, however, and Quade peered inside.

After a moment he reached in and drew out a rifle. He took it over to a nearby rock, smashed the gun's breech, then flung it, useless, aside. Returning to the borer, he again peered in.

Sue was about to scream from the torturous suspense when he at last straightened up and looked around at the white-faced girl and her father.

"Mr. Holmes is tougher than I'd thought possible," he said, with a thin smile; "he's still alive." And, as Sue gasped with relief, he added: "Would you like to see him?"

He dragged the young man's unconscious body roughly out on the floor. There were several bad bruises on his face and head, but otherwise he was apparently uninjured. As Quade stood over him, playing idly with the automatic, he stirred, and blinked, and at last, with an effort, got up on one elbow and looked straight at the thin lips and narrowed eyes of the man standing above. He shook his head, trying to comprehend, then muttered hazily:

"You—you're—Quade?"

Quade did not have time to answer, for Sue Guinness cried out:

"Phil! Are you all right?"

Phil stared stupidly around, caught sight of the two who lay bound on the floor, and staggered to his feet. "Sue!" he cried, relief and understanding flooding his voice. He started towards her.

"Stand where you are!" Quade snapped harshly, and the automatic in his hand came up. Holmes peered at it and stopped, but his blood-streaked face settled into tight lines, and his body tensed.

"You'd better," continued Quade. "Now tell me what happened to Juan."

Phil forced himself to be calm. "Your pal, the greaser?" he said cuttingly. "He's lying on a bunk in your shack. He shot himself, playing with a gun."

Quade chose not to notice the way Phil said this, but a little of the suave self-confidence was gone from his face as he said: "Well, in that case I'll have to hurry back to the surface to attend to him. But don't be alarmed," he added, more brightly. "I'll be back for you all in an hour or so."

At this, David Guinness struggled frantically with his bonds and yelled:

"Don't believe him, Phil! He's going to leave us here, to starve and die! He told us so just before you came down!"

Quade's face twitched perceptibly. His eyes were nervous.

"Is that true, Quade?" Holmes asked. There was a steely note in his voice.

"Why—no, of course not," the other said hastily, uncertain whether to lie or not. "Of course I didn't!"

Phil Holmes looked square into his eyes. He bluffed.

"You couldn't desert us, Quade. You haven't the guts. You haven't the guts."

His face and eyes burned with the contempt that was in his words. It cut Quade to the raw. But he could not avoid Phil's eyes. He stared at them for a full moment, trembling slightly. Slowly, by inches, he started to back toward the sphere; then suddenly he ran for it with all his might, Holmes after him. Quade got to it first, and inside, as he yanked in the searchlight and slammed and locked the door, he yelled:

"You'll see, you damned pup! You'll see!" And there was the smothered sound of half-maniacal laughter....

Phil threw all his weight against the metal door, but it was hopeless and he knew it. He had gathered himself for another rush when he heard Guinness yell:

"Back, Phil—back! He'll turn on the side disintegrators!"

Mad with rage as the young man was, he at once saw the danger and leaped away—only to almost fall over the professor's prone body. With hurrying, trembling fingers he untied the pair's bonds, and they struggled to their feet, cramped and stiff. Then it was Phil who warned them.

"Back as far as you can! Hurry!" He grabbed Sue's hand and plunged toward the uncertain protection of a huge rock far in the rear. At once he made them lie flat on the ground.

As yet the sphere had not stirred nor emitted a whisper of sound, though they knew the man inside was conning the controls in a fever of haste to leave the cavern. But they hadn't long to wait. There came a sputter, a starting cough from the rocket tubes beneath the sphere. Quickly they warmed into life, and the dully glimmering ball rocked in the hole it lay in. Then a cataract of noise unleashed itself; a devastating thunder roared through the echoing cavern as the rockets burst into full force. A wave of brilliant orange-red splashed out from under the sphere, licked back up its sides, and seemed literally to shove the great ball up towards the hole in the ceiling.

Its ascent was very slow. As it gained height it looked—save for its speed—like a fantastic meteor flaming through the night, for the orange plumage that streamed from beneath lit the ball with dazzling color. A glowing sphere, it staggered midway between floor and ceiling, creeping jerkily upwards.

"He's not going to hit the hole!" shouted Guinness.

The borer had not risen in a perfectly straight line; it jarred against the rim of the hole, and wavered uncertainly. Every second the roar of its rockets, swollen by echoes, rose in a savage crescendo; the faces of the three who watched were painted orange in the glow.

The sphere was blind. The man inside could judge his course only by the feel. As the three who were deserted watched, hoping ardently that Quade would not be able to find the opening, the left side-rockets spouted lances of fire, and they knew he had discovered the way to maneuver the borer laterally. The new flames welded with the exhaust of the main tubes into a great fan-shaped tail, so brilliant and shot through with other colors that their eyes could not stand the sight, except in winks. The borer jerked to the right, but still it could not find the hole. Then the flames lessened for a moment, and the borer sank down, to rise again a moment later. Its ascent was so labored that Phil shouted to Professor Guinness:

"Why so slow?"

And the inventor told him that which he had not seen for the intolerable light.

"Only half his rockets are on!"

This time the sphere was correctly aimed, however, and it roared straight into the hole. Immediately the fierce sound of the exhaust was muffled, and in a few seconds only the fiery plumage, shooting down from the ceiling, showed where the machine was. Then this disappeared, and the noise alone was left.

Phil leaped forward, intending to stare up, but Guinness's yell halted him.

"Not yet! He might still use the disintegrators!"

For many minutes they waited, till the muffled exhaust had died to a drone. There was a puzzled expression on the professor's face as the three at last walked over and dared peer up into the hole. Far above, the splash of orange lit the walls of the tunnel.

"That's funny!" the old man muttered. "He's only using half the rockets—about ten. I thought he'd turn them all on when he got into the hole, but he didn't. Either they were damaged in the fall, or Quade doesn't see fit to use them."

"Half of them are enough," said Phil bitterly, and put his arm around the quiet girl standing next to him. Together, a silent little group, they watched the spot of orange die to a pin-point; watched it waver, twinkle, ever growing smaller.... And then it was gone.

Gone! Back to the surface of the earth, to the normal world of reality. Only four miles above them—a small enough distance on the surface itself—and yet it might have been a million miles, so utterly were they barred from it....

The same thought was in their minds, though none of them dared express it. They were thinking of the serene desert, and the cool wind, and the buttes and the high hills, placid in the moonlight. Of the hushed rise of the dawn, the first flush of the sun that was so achingly lovely on the desert. The sun they would never see again, buried in a lifeless world of gloom four miles within.... And buried alive—and not alive for long....

But that way lay madness. Phil Holmes drove the horrible thoughts from his brain and forced a smile to his face.

"Well, that's that!" he said in a voice meant to be cheerful.

The dim cavern echoed his words mockingly. With the earth-borer gone—the man-made machine that had dared break a solitude undisturbed since the earth first cooled—the great cavern seemed to return to its awful original mood. The three dwarfed humans became wholly conscious of it. They felt it almost a living thing, stretching vastly around them, tightening its unheard spell on them. Its smell, of mouldy earth and rocks down which water slowly dripped, filled their nostrils and somehow added to their fear.

As they looked about, their eyes became accustomed to the dim, eery, phosphorescent illumination. They saw little worm-like creatures now and again appear from tiny holes between stalagmites in the jagged floor; and, as Phil wondered in his mind how long it would be before they would be reduced to using them for food, a strange mole-sized animal scraped from the darkness and pecked at one of them. As it slithered away, a writhing shape in its mouth, Holmes muttered bitterly: "A competitor!" Vague, flitting forms haunted the gloom among the stalactites of the distorted ceiling—hints of the things that lived in the terrible silence of this nether world. Here Time had paused, and life had halted in primate form.

A little moan came from Sue Guinness's pale lips. She plucked at her arm; a sickly white worm, only an inch long, had fallen on it from the ceiling. "Oh!" she gasped. "Oh!"

Phil drew her closer to him, and walked with her over to Quade's wrecked borer. "Let's see what we've got here," he suggested cheerfully.

The machine was over on its side, the metal mangled and crushed beyond repair. Nevertheless, he squeezed into it. "Stand back!" he warned. "I'm going to try its rockets!" There was a click of broken machinery, and that was all. "Rockets gone," Phil muttered.

He pulled another lever over. There was a sputter from within the borer, then a furious roar that sent great echoes beating through the cavern. A cloud of dust reared up before the bottom of the machine, whipped madly for a moment, and sank as the bellow of sound died down. Sue saw that a rocky rise in the floor directly in front of the disintegrators had been planed off levelly.

Phil scrambled out. "The disintegrators work," he said, "but a lot of good they do us. The borer's hopelessly cracked." He shrugged his shoulders, and with a discouraged gesture cast to the ground a coil of rope he had found inside.

Then suddenly he swung around. "Professor!" he called to the old figure standing bowed beneath the hole in the ceiling. "There's a draft blowing from somewhere! Do you feel it?"

Guinness felt with his hands a moment and nodded slowly. "Yes," he said.

"It's coming from this way!" Sue said excitedly, pointing into the darkness on one side of the cavern. "And it goes up the hole we made in the ceiling!"

Phil turned eagerly to the old inventor. "It must come from somewhere," he said, "and that somewhere may take us toward the surface. Let's follow it!"

"We might as well," the other agreed wearily. His was the tone of a man who has only a certain time to live.

But Phil was more eager. "While there's life, there's hope," he said cheerfully. "Come on, Sue, Professor!" And he led the way forward toward the dim, distorted rock shapes in the distance.

The roof and sides of the cavern angled down into a rough, tunnel-like opening, from which the draft swept. It was a heavy air, weighted with the smell of moist earth and lifeless water and a nameless, flat, stale gas. They slowly made their way through the impeding stalagmites, surrounded by a dark blur of shadows, the ghostly phosphorescent light illuminating well only the few rods around them. Utter silence brooded over the tunnel.

Phil paused when they had gone about seventy-five feet. "I left that rope behind," he said, "and we may need it. I'll return and get it, and you both wait right here." With the words he turned and went back into the shadows.

He went as fast as he could, not liking to leave the other two alone. But when he had retrieved the rope and tied it to his waist, he permitted himself a last look up as he passed under the hole in the ceiling—and what he saw there tensed every muscle in his body, and made his heart beat like mad. Again there was a tiny spot of orange in the blackness above!

"Professor!" he yelled excitedly. "Sue! Come here! The sphere's coming back!"

There was no doubt about it. The pin-point of light was growing each second, with the flame of the descending exhausts. Guinness and his daughter ran from the tunnel, and, guided by Phil's excited ejaculations, hurried to his side. Their eyes confirmed what his had seen. The earth-borer was coming down!

"But," Guinness said bewilderedly, "those rockets were enough to lift him!"

This was a mystery. Even though ten rockets were on—ten tiny spots of orange flame—the sphere came down swiftly. The same force which some time before had lifted it slowly up was now insufficient. The roar of the tubes rose rapidly. "Get back!" Phil ordered, remembering the danger, and they all retreated to the mouth of the tunnel, ready to peep cautiously around the edge. Holmes' jaws were locked tight with grim resolution. Quade was coming back! he told himself exultantly. This time he must not go up alone! This time—!

But his half-formed resolutions were idle. He could not know what frightful thing was bringing Quade down—what frightful experience was in store for them all....

CHAPTER IV

Spawn of the Cavern

In a crescendo of noise that stunned their ears, the earth-borer came down. Tongues of fire flared from the hole, speared to the ground and were deflected upward, cradling the metal ball in a wave of flame. Through this fiery curtain the machine slowly lowered to the floor, where a shower of sparks spattered out, blinding the eyes of the watchers with their brilliance. For a full minute the orange-glowing sphere lay there, quivering from the vibration; then the exhausts died and the wave of flame wavered and sank into nothingness. While their ear-drums continued the thunder, the three stared at the borer, not daring to approach, yet striving to solve the mystery of why it had sunk despite the up-thrust of ten rocket tubes.

As their eyes again became accustomed to the familiar phosphorescent illumination, pallid and cold after the fierce orange flame, they saw why— and their eyes went wide with surprise and horror.

A strange mass was covering the top of the earth-borer—something that looked like a heap of viscid, whitish jelly. It was sprawled shapelessly over the round upper part of the metal sphere, a half-transparent, loathsome stuff, several feet thick in places.

And Phil Holmes, striving to understand what it could be, saw an awful thing. "It's moving!" he whispered, unconsciously drawing Sue closer. "There's— there's life in it!"

Lazy quiverings were running through the mound of jelly, pulsings that gave evidence of its low organism. They saw little ripples of even beat run over it, and under them steady, sluggish convulsions that told of life; that showed, perhaps, that the thing was hungry and preparing to move its body in quest of food.

It was alive, unquestionably. The borer lay still, but this thing moved internally, of itself. It was life in its lowest, most primate form. The mass was mind, stomach, muscle and body all in one, stark and raw before their startled eyes.

"Oh, God!" Phil whispered through the long pause. "It can't be real!..."

"Protoplasm—a monster amoeba," David Guinness's curiously cracked voice said. "Just as it exists on the surface, only microscopically. Primate life...."

The lock of the earth-borer clicked. Phil gasped. "Quade is coming out!" he said. A little cry of horror came from Sue. And the metal door opened.

James Quade stepped through, automatic in hand. He was fresh from the light inside, and he could not see well. He was quite unconscious of what was oozing down on him from above, of the flabby heap that was carefully stretching down for him. He peered into the gloom, looking for the three he had deserted, and all the time an arm from the mass above crept nearer. Sue

Guinness's nerves suddenly gave, and she shrieked; but Quade's ears were deaf from the borer's thunder, and he did not hear her.

It was when he lifted one foot back into the sphere—probably to get out the searchlight—that he felt the thing's presence. He looked up—and a strange sound came from him. For seconds he apparently could not move, stark fear rooting him to the ground, the gun limp in his hand.

Then a surge ran through the mound of flesh, and the arm, a pseudopod, reached more rapidly for him.

It stung Quade into action. He leaped back, brought up his automatic, and fired at the thing once; then three times more. He, and each one of the others, saw four bullets thud into the heap of pallid matter and heard them clang on the metal of the sphere beneath. They had gone right through its flesh—but they showed no slightest effect!

Quade was evidently unwilling to leave the sphere. Jerking his arm up he brought his trigger finger back again. A burst of three more shots barked through the cavern, echoing and re-echoing. The man screamed an inarticulate oath as he saw how useless his bullets were, and hurled the empty gun at the monster—which was down on the floor now, and bunching its sluggish body together.

The automatic went right into it. They could all see it there, in the middle of the amorphous body, while the creature stopped, as if determining whether or not it was food. Quade screwed his courage together in the pause, and tried to dodge past to the door of the sphere; but the monster was alert: another pseudopod sprang out from its shapeless flesh, sending him back on his heels.

The feeler had all but touched Quade, and with the closeness of his escape, the remnants of his courage gave. He yelled, and turned and ran.

He ran straight for the three who watched from the tunnel mouth, and the mound of shapeless jelly came fast on his trail. It came in surging rolls, like thick fluid oozing forward; it would have been hard to measure its size, for each moment it changed. The only impression the four humans had was that of a wave of half-transparent matter that one instant was a sticky ball of viscid flesh and the next a rapidly advancing crescent whose horns reached far out on each flank to cut off retreat.

By instinct Phil jerked Sue around and yelled at the professor to run, for the old man seemed to be frozen into an attitude of fearful interest. Bullets would not stop the thing—could anything? Holmes wondered. He could visualize all too easily the death they would meet if that shapeless, naked protoplasmic mass overtook and flowed over them....

But he wasted no time with such thoughts. They ran, all three, into the dark tunnel.

Quade caught up with them quickly. Personal enmity was suspended before this common peril. They could not run at full speed, for a multitude of obstacles hindered them. Tortuous ridges of rock lay directly across their path, formations that had been whipped in some mad, eon-old convulsion and then, through the ages, remained frozen into their present distortion; black pits gaped suddenly before them; half-seen stalagmites, whose crystalline edges were razor-sharp, tore through to their flesh. Haste was perilous where every moment they might stumble into an unseen cleft and go pitching into awful depths below. They were staking everything on the draft that blew steadily in their faces; Phil told himself desperately that it must lead to some opening—it must!

But what if the opening were a vertical, impassable tunnel? He would not think of that....

Old David Guinness tired fast, and was already lagging in the rear when Quade gasped hoarsely:

"Hurry! It's close behind!"

Surging rapidly at a constant distance behind them, it came on. It was as fast as they were, and evidently untiring. It was in its own element; obstacles meant nothing to it. It oozed over the jagged ridges that took the humans precious moments to scramble past, and the speed of its weird progress seemed to increase as theirs faltered. It was a heartless mass driven inexorably by primal instinct towards the food that lay ahead. The dim phosphorescent illumination tinged its flabby tissues a weird white.

The passage they stumbled through narrowed. Long irregular spears of stalactites hung from the unseen ceiling; others, the drippings of ages, pronged up from the floor, shredding their clothes as they jarred into them. One moment they were clambering up-hill, slipping on the damp rock; the next they were sliding down into unprobed darkness, reckless of where they would land. They were aware only that the water-odorous draft was still in their faces, and the hungry mound of flesh behind....

"I can't last much longer!" old Guinness's winded voice gasped. "Best leave me behind. I—I might delay it!"

For answer, Phil went back, grabbed him by the arm and dragged his tired body forward. He was snatching a glance behind to see how close the monster was, when Sue's frightened voice reached him from ahead.

"There's a wall here, Phil—and no way through!"

And then Holmes came to it. It barred the passage, and was apparently unbroken. Yet the draft still came!

"Search for where the draft enters!" he yelled. "You take that side!" And he started feeling over the clammy, uneven surface, searching frantically for a cleft. It seemed to be hopeless. Quade stood staring back into the gloom, his eyes looking for what he knew was surging towards them. His face had gone sickly white, he was trembling as if with fever, and he sucked in air with long, racking gasps.

"Here! I have it!" cried the girl suddenly at her end of the wall. The other three ran over, and saw, just above her head, a narrow rift in the rock, barely wide enough to squirm through. "Into it!" Phil ordered tersely. He grasped her, raised her high, and she wormed through. Quade scrambled to get in next, but Holmes shoved him aside and boosted the old man through. Then he helped the other.

A second after he had swung himself up, a wave of whitish matter rolled up below, hungry pseudopods reaching for the food it knew was near. It began to trickle up the wall....

The crack was narrow and jagged; utterly black. Phil could hear Quade frantically worming himself ahead, and he wondered achingly if it would lead anywhere. Then a faint, clear voice from ahead rang out:

"It's opening up!"

Sue's voice! Phil breathed more easily. The next moment Quade scrambled through; dim light came; and they were in another vast, ghostly-lit cavern

The crack came out on its floor-level; Guinness was resting near, and his daughter had her hands on a large boulder of rock. "Let's shove it against the hole!" she suggested to Phil. "It might stop it!"

"Good, Sue, good!" he exclaimed, and at once all four of them strained at the chunk, putting forth every bit of strength they had. The boulder stirred, rolled over, and thudded neatly in front of the crack, almost completely sealing it. There was only a cleft of five inches on one side.

But their expression of relief died in their throats. A tiny trickle of white appeared through the niche. The amorphous monster was compressing itself to a single stream, thin enough to squeeze through even that narrow space.

They could not block it. They had nothing to attack it with. There was nothing to do but run.... And hope for a chance to double back....

As nearly as they could make out, this second cavern was as large as the first. They could dimly see the fantastic shapes of hundreds of stalactites hanging from the ceiling. Clumps of stalagmites made the floor a maze which they threaded painfully. The strong steady draft guided them like a radio beacon, leading them to their only faint hope of escape and life. Guinness, very tired, staggered along mechanically, a heavy weight on Phil's supporting arm; James Quade ran here and there in frantic spurts of speed. Sue was silent, but the hopelessness in her eyes tortured Phil like a wound. His shirt had long since been ripped to shreds; his face, bruised in the first place by the borer he had crashed in, now was scratched and bloody from contact with rough stalagmites.

Then, without warning, they suddenly found among the rough walls on the far side of the cavern, the birthplace of the draft. It lay at the edge of the floor—a dark hole, very wide. Black, sinister and clammy from the draft that poured from it, it pierced vertically down into the very bowels of the earth. It was impassable.

James Quade crumpled at the brink; "It's the end!" he moaned. "We can't go farther! It's the end of the draft!"

The hole blocked their forward path completely. They could not go ahead.... In seconds, it seemed, the slithering that told of the monster's approach sounded from behind. Sue's eyes were already fixed on the awful, surging mass when a voice off to one side yelled:

"Here! Quick!"

It was Phil Holmes. He had been scouting through the gloom, and had found something.

The other three ran to him. "There's another draft going through here," he explained rapidly, pointing to an angled crevice in the rocky wall. "There's a good chance it goes to the cavern where the sphere and the hole to the surface are. Anyway, we've got to take it. I'd better go first, after this—and you, Quade, last. I trust you less than the monster behind."

He turned and edged into the crack, and the others followed as he had ordered. Quickly the passageway broadened, and they found the going much easier than it had been before. For perhaps ten minutes they scrambled along, with the draft always on their backs and the blessed, though faint, fire of hope kindling again. In all that time they did not see their pursuer once, and the hope that they had lost it brought a measure of much needed optimism to drive their tired bodies onward. They found but few time-wasting obstacles. If only the tunnel would continue right into the original cavern! If only their path would stay clear and unhindered!

But it did not. The sound of Phil's footsteps ahead stopped, and when Sue and her father came up they saw why.

"A river!" Phil said.

They were standing on a narrow ledge that overhung an underground river. A fetid smell of age-old, lifeless water rose from it. Dimly, at least fifty feet across, they could see the other side, shrouded in vague shadows. The inky stream beneath did not seem to move at all, but remained smooth and hard and thick-looking.

They could not go around it. The ledge was only a few feet wide, and blocked at each side.

"Got to cross!" Phil said tersely.

Quade, sickly-faced, stared down. "There—there might be other things in that water!" he gasped. "Monsters!"

"Sure," agreed Phil contemptuously. "You'd better stay here." He turned to the others. "I'll see how deep it is," he said, and without the faintest hesitation dove flatly in.

Oily ripples washed back, and they saw his head poke through, sputtering. "Not deep," he said. "Chest-high. Come on."

He reached for Sue, helped her down, and did the same for her father. Holding each by the hand, Sue's head barely above the water, he started across. They had not gone more than twenty feet when they heard Quade, left on the bank, give a hoarse yell of fear and dive into the water. Their dread pursuer had caught up with them.

And it followed—on the water! Phil had hoped it would not be able to cross, but once more the thing's astounding adaptability dashed his hopes. Without hesitation, the whitish jelly sprawled out over the water, rolling after them with ghastly, snake-like ripples, its pallid body standing out gruesomely against the black, odorous tide.

Quade came up thrashing madly, some feet to the side of the other three. He was swimming—and swimming with such strength that he quickly left them behind. He would be across before they; and that meant there was a good chance that the earth-borer would go up again with only one passenger....

Phil fought against the water, pulling Sue and her father forward as best he could. From behind came the rippling sound of their shapeless pursuer. "Ten feet more—" Holmes began—then abruptly stopped.

There had been a swish, a ripple upstream. And as their heads turned they saw the water part and a black head, long, evil, glistening, pointing coldly down to where they were struggling towards the shore. Phil Holmes felt his strength ooze out. He heard Professor Guinness gasp:

"A water-snake!"

Its head was reared above the surface, gliding down on them silently, leaving a wedge of long, sluggish ripples behind. When thirty feet away the glistening head dipped under, and a great half-circle of leg-thick body arched out. It was like an oily stream of curved cable; then it ended in a pointed tail—and the creature was entirely under water....

With desperate strength Phil hauled the girl to the bank and, standing in several feet of water, pushed her up. Then he whirled and yanked old Guinness past him up into the hands of his daughter. With them safe, and Sue reaching out her hand for him, he began to scramble up himself.

But he was too late. There was a swish in the water behind him, and toothless, hard-gummed jaws clamped tight over one leg and drew him back and under. And with the touch of the creature's mouth a stiff shock jolted him; his body went numb; his arms flopped limply down. He was paralyzed.

Sue Guinness cried out. Her father stared helplessly at the spot where his young partner had disappeared with so little commotion.

"It was an eel," he muttered dully. "Some kind of electric eel...."

Phil dimly realized the same thing. A moment later his face broke the surface, but he could not cry out; he could not move his little finger. Only his involuntary muscles kept working—his heart and his lungs. He found he could control his breathing a little.... And then he was wondering why he was remaining motionless on the surface. Gradually he came to understand.

He had not felt it, but the eel had let go its hold on his leg, and had disappeared. But only for a moment. Suddenly, from somewhere near, its gleaming body writhed crazily, and a terrific twist of its tail hit Phil a glancing blow on the chest. He was swept under, and the water around him became a maelstrom. When next he bobbed to the tumultuous surface, he managed to get a much-needed breath of air—and in the swirling currents glimpsed the long, snake-like head of the eel go shooting by, with thin trickles of stuff that looked like white jelly clinging to it.

That explained what was happening. The eel had been challenged by the ameboid monster, and they were fighting for possession of him—the common prey.

The water became an inferno of whipping and lashing movements, of whitish fibers and spearing thrusts of a glistening black electric body. Unquestionably the eel was using its numbing electric shock on its foe. Time and time again Phil felt the amoeba grasp him, searingly, only to be wrenched free by the force of the currents the combat stirred up. Once he thudded into the bottom of the river, and his lungs seemed about to burst before he was again shot to the top and managed to get a breath. At last the water quieted somewhat, and Phil, at the surface, saw the eel bury its head in a now apathetic mound of flesh.

It tore a portion loose with savage jaws, a portion that still writhed after it was separated from the parent mass; and then the victor glided swiftly downstream, and disappeared under the surface....

Holmes floated helplessly on the inky water. He could see the amoeba plainly; it was still partly paralyzed, for it was very still. But then a faint tremor ran through it; a wave ran over its surface—and it moved slowly towards him once again.

Desperately Phil tried to retreat. The will was there, but the body would not work. Save for a feeble flutter of his hands and feet, he could not move. He could not even turn around to bid Sue and David Guinness good-by—with his eyes....

Then a fresh, loved voice sounded just behind him, and he felt something tighten around his waist.

"It's all right, dear!" the voice called. "Hang on; we'll get you out!"

Sue had come in after him! She had grasped the rope tied to his belt, and she and her father were pulling him back to the bank!

He wanted to tell her to go back—the amoeba was only feet away—but he could only manage a little croak. And then he was safe up on the ledge at the other side of the river.

A surge of strength filled his limbs, and he knew the shock was rapidly wearing off. But it was also wearing off of the monster in the water. Its speed increased; the ripplings of its amorphous body-substance became quicker, more excited. It came on steadily.

While it came, the girl and her father worked desperately over Phil, massaging his body and pulling him further up the bank. It had all but reached the bank when Holmes gasped:

"I think I can walk now. Where—where did Quade go to?"

Guinness gestured over to the right, up a dim winding passage through the rocks.

"Then we must follow—fast!" Phil said, staggering to his feet. "He may get to the sphere first; he'll go up by himself even yet! I'm all right!"

Despite his words, he could not run, and could only command an awkward walk. Sue lifted one of his arms around her shoulder, and her father took the other, and without a backward glance they labored ahead. But Phil's strength quickly returned, and they raised the pace until they had broken once more into a stumbling run.

How far ahead James Quade was, they did not know, but obviously they could follow where he had gone. Once again the draft was strong on their backs. They felt sure they were on the last stretch, headed for the earth-borer. But, unless they could overtake Quade, he would be there first. They had no illusions about what that would mean....

CHAPTER V

A Death More Hideous

Quade was there first.

When they burst out of a narrow crevice, not far from the funnel-shaped opening they had originally entered, they saw him standing beside the open door of the sphere as if waiting. The searchlight inside was still on, and in its shaft of light they could see that he was smiling thinly, once more his old, confident self. It would only take him a second to jump in, slam the door and lock it. He could afford a last gesture....

The three stopped short. They saw something he did not.

"So!" he observed in his familiar, mocking voice. He paused, seeing that they did not come on. He had plenty of time.

He said something else, but the two men and the girl did not hear what it was. As if by a magnet their eyes were held by what was hanging above him, clinging to the lip of the hole the sphere had made in the ceiling.

It was an amoeba, another of those single-celled, protoplasmic mounds of flesh. It had evidently come down through the hole; and now it was stretching, rubber-like, lower and lower, a living, reaching stalactite of whitish hunger.

Quade was all unconscious of it. His final words reached Phil's consciousness.

"... And this time, of course, I will keep the top disintegrators on. No other monster will then be able to weigh me down!"

He shrugged his shoulders and turned to the door. And that movement was the signal that brought his doom. Without a sound, the poised mass above dropped.

James Quade never knew what hit him. The heap of whitish jelly fell squarely. There was a brief moment of frantic lashing, of tortured struggles—then only tiny ripples running through the monster as it fed.

Sue Guinness turned her head. But the two men for some reason could not take their eyes away....

It was the girl's voice that jerked them back to reality. "The other!" she gasped. "It's coming, behind!"

They had completely forgotten the mass in the tunnel. Turning, they saw that it was only fifteen feet away and approaching fast, and instinctively they ran out into the cavern, skirting the sphere widely. When they came to Quade's wrecked borer Phil, who had snatched a glance behind, dragged them down behind it. For he had seen their pursuer abandon the chase and go to share in the meal of its fellow.

"We'd best not get too far away," he whispered. "When they leave the front of the borer, maybe we can make a dash for it."

For minutes that went like hours the young man watched, waiting for the creatures to be done, hoping that they would go away. Fortunately the sphere lay between, and he was not forced to see too much. Only one portion of one of the monsters was visible, lapping out from behind the machine....

At last his body tensed, and he gripped Sue and her father's arm in quick warning. The things were leaving the sphere. Or, rather, only one was. For Phil saw that they had agglutenated—merged into oneness—and now the monster that remained was the sum of the sizes of the original two. And more....

They all watched. And they all saw the amoeba stop, hesitate for a moment—and come straight for the wrecked borer behind which they were hidden.

"Damn!" Phil whispered hoarsely. "It's still hungry—and it's after us!"

David Guinness sighed wearily. "It's heavy and sluggish, now," he said, "so maybe if we run again.... Though I don't know how I can last any longer...."

Holmes did not answer. His eyes were narrowed; he was casting about desperately for a plan. He hardly felt Sue's light touch on his arm as she whispered:

"In case, Phil—in case.... This must be good-by...."

But the young man turned to her with gleaming eyes. "Good-by, nothing!" he cried. "We've still got a card to play!"

She stared at him, wondering if he had cracked from the strain of what he had passed through. But his next words assured her he had not. "Go back, Sue," he said levelly. "Go far back. We'll win through this yet."

She hesitated, then obeyed. She crept back from the wrecked borer, back into the dim rear, eyes on Phil and the sluggish mass that moved inexorably towards him. When she had gone fifteen or twenty yards she paused, and watched the two men anxiously.

Phil was talking swiftly to Professor Guinness. His voice was low and level, and though she could not hear the words she could catch the tone of assurance that ran through them. She saw her father nod his head, and he seemed to make the gesture with vigor. "I will," she heard him say; and he slapped Phil on the back, adding: "But for God's sake, be careful!"

And with these words the old man wormed inside Quade's wrecked borer and was gone from the girl's sight.

She wanted desperately to run forward and learn what Phil intended to do, but she restrained herself and obeyed his order. She waited, and watched; and saw the young man stand up, look at the slowly advancing monster—and deliberately walk right into its path!

Sue could not move from her fright. In a daze she saw Phil advance cautiously towards the amoeba and pause when within five feet of it. The thing stopped; remained absolutely motionless. She saw him take another short step forward. This time a pseudopod emerged, and reached slowly out for him. Phil avoided it easily, but by so narrow a margin that the girl's heart stopped beating. Then she saw him step back; and, snail-like, the creature followed, pausing twice, as if wary and suspicious. Slowly Phil Holmes drew it after him.

To Sue, who did not know what was his plan, it seemed a deliberate invitation to death. She forgot about her father, lying inside the mangled borer, waiting. She did not see that Phil was leading the monster directly in front of it....

It was a grotesque, silent pursuit. The creature appeared to be unalert; its movements were sloth-like; yet the girl knew that if Phil once ventured an inch too close, or slipped, or tried to dodge past it to the sphere, its torpidness would vanish and it would have him. His maneuvering had to be delicate, judged to a matter of inches. Tense with the suspense, the strain of the slow-paced seconds, she watched—and yet hardly dared to watch, fearful of the awful thing she might see.

It was a fantastic game of tag her lover was playing, with death the penalty for tardiness. The slow, enticing movements were repeated again and again, Phil advancing very close, and stepping back in the nick of time. Always he barely avoided the clutching white arms that were extended, and little by little he decoyed the thing onward....

Then came the end. As Holmes was almost in front of the wrecked machine, Sue saw him glance quickly aside—and, as if waiting for that moment when he would be off guard, the monster whipped forward in a great, reaching surge.

Sue's ragged nerves cracked: she shrieked. They had him! She started forward, then halted abruptly. With a tremendous leap, Phil Holmes had wrenched free and flung himself backwards. She heard his yell:

"Now!"

There was a sputter from the bottom of the outstretched borer; then, like the crack of a whip, came a bellow of awful sound.

A thick cloud of dust reared up, and the ear-numbing thunder rolled through the cavern in great pulsing echoes. And then Sue Guinness understood what the young man had been about.

The disintegrators of James Quade's borer had sent a broad beam of annihilation into the monster. His own machine had destroyed his destroyer—and given his intended victims their only chance to escape from the dread fate he had schemed for them.

Sue could see no trace of the creature in its pyre of slow-swirling dust. Caught squarely, its annihilation had been utter. And then, through the thunder that still echoed in her ear-drums, she heard a joyful voice.

"We got 'em!"

Through the dusty haze Phil appeared at her side. He flung his arms up exultantly, swept her off the ground, hugged her close.

"We got 'em!" he cried again. "We're free—free to go up!"

Professor David Guinness crawled from the borer. His face, for the first time since the descent, wore a broad smile. Phil ran over to him, slapped him on the back; and the older man said:

"You did it beautifully, Phil." He turned to Sue. "He had to decoy them right in front of the disintegrators. It was—well, it was magnificent!"

"All credit to Sue: she was my inspiration!" Phil said, laughing. "But now," he added, "let's see if we can fix those dead rocket-tubes. I have a patient up above—and, anyway, I'm not over-fond of this place!"

The three had won through. They had blasted four miles down from the surface of the earth. The brain of an elderly scientist, the quick-witted courage of a young engineer, had achieved the seemingly impossible—and against obstacles that could not have been predicted. Death had attended that achievement, as death often does accompany great forward steps; James Quade had gone to a death more hideous than that he devised for the others. But, in spite of the justice of it, a moment of silence fell on the three survivors as they came to the spot where his fate at last had caught up to him.

But it was only a moment. It was relieved by Professor Guinness's picking up the chunk of radium ore his former partner had hewn from the cavern's wall. He held it up for all to see, and smiled.

"Here it is," he said simply.

Then he led the way into his earth-borer, and the little door closed quietly and firmly into place.

For a few minutes slight tappings came from within, as if a wrench or a screwdriver were being used. Then the tappings stopped, and all was silence.

A choke, a starting cough, came from beneath the sphere. A torrent of rushing sound burst out, and spears of orange flame spurted from the bottom and splashed up its sides, bathing it in fierce, brilliant light. It stirred. Then, slowly and smoothly, the great ball of metal raised up.

It hit the edge of the hole in the ceiling, and hung there, hesitating. Side-rockets flared, and the sphere angled over. Then it slid, roaring, through the hole.

Swiftly the spots of orange from its rocket-tube exhausts died to pin-points. There were now almost twenty of them. And soon these pin-points wavered, and vanished utterly.

Then there was only blackness in the hole that went up to the surface. Blackness in the hole, calm night on the desert above—and silence, as if the cavern were brooding on the puny figures and strange machines that had for the first time dared invade its solitude, in the realms four miles within the earth....

The monster emanated power, sinister, malevolent power.

THE LAKE OF LIGHT

By Jack Williamson

In the frozen wastes at the bottom of the world two explorers find a strange pool of white fire—and have a strange adventure.

The roar of the motor rang loud in the frosty air above a desert of ice. The sky above us was a deep purple-blue; the red sun hung like a crimson eye low in the north. Three thousand feet below, through a hazy blue mist of wind-whipped, frozen vapor, was the rugged wilderness of black ice-peaks and blizzard-carved hummocks of snow—a grim, undulating waste, black and yellow, splotched with crystal white. The icy wind howled dismally through the struts. We were flying above the weird ice-mountains of the Enderby quadrant of Antarctica.

That was a perilous flight, across the blizzard-whipped bottom of the world. In all the years of polar exploration by air, since Byrd's memorable flights, this area had never been crossed. The intrepid Britisher, Major Meriden, with the daring American aviatrix whom the world had known as Mildred Cross before she married him, had flown into it nineteen years before—and like many others they had never returned.

Faintly, above the purring drone of the motor, I heard Ray Summers' shout. I drew my gaze from the desolate plateau of ice below and leaned forward. His lean, fur-hooded face was turned back toward me. A mittened hand was pointing, and thin lips moved in words that I did not hear above the roar of the engine and the scream of the wind.

I turned and looked out to the right, past the shimmering silver disk of the propeller. Under the blue haze of ice-crystals in the air, the ice lay away in a vast undulating plain of black and yellow, broken with splotches of prismatic whiteness, lying away in frozen desolation to the rim of the cold violet sky. Rising against that sky I saw a curious thing.

It was a mountain of fire!

Beyond the desert of ice, a great conical peak pointed straight into the amethystine gloom of the polar heavens. It was brilliantly white, a finger of milky fire, a sharp cone of pure light. It shone with white radiance. It was brighter, far brighter, than is the sacred cone of Fujiyama in the vivid day of Japan.

For many minutes I stared in wonder at it. Far away it was; it looked very small. It was like a little heap of light poured from the hand of a fire-god. What it might be, I could not imagine. At first sight, I imagined it might be a volcano with streams of incandescent lava flowing down the side. I knew that this continent of mystery boasted Mt. Erebus and other active craters. But there was none of the smoke or lurid yellow flame which accompanies volcanic eruptions.

I was still watching it, and wondering, when the catastrophe took place—the catastrophe which hurled us into a mad extravaganza of amazing adventure.

Our little two-place amphibian was flying smoothly, through air unusually good for this continent of storms. The twelve cylinders of the motor had been firing regularly since we took off from Byrd's old station at Little America fifteen hours before. We had crossed the pole in safety. It looked as if we might succeed in this attempt to penetrate the last white spot on the map. Then it Happened.

A sudden crack of snapping metal rang out sharp as a pistol report. A bright blade of metal flashed past the wing-struts, to fall in a flashing arc. The motor broke abruptly into a mad, deep-voiced roar. Terrific vibration shook the ship, until I feared that it would go to pieces.

Ray Summers, with his usual quick efficiency, cut the throttle. Quickly the motor slowed to idling speed; the vibration stopped. A last cough of the engine, and there was no sound save the shrill screaming of the wind in the gloomy twilight of this unknown land beyond the pole.

"What in the devil!" I exclaimed.

"The prop! See!" Ray pointed ahead.

I looked, and the dreadful truth flashed upon me. The steel propeller was gone, or half of it at least. One blade was broken off at a jagged line just above the hub.

"The propeller! What made it break? I've never heard—"

"Search me!" Ray grinned. "The important thing is that it did. It was all-metal, of course, tested and guaranteed. The guarantee isn't worth much here. A flaw in the forging, perhaps, that escaped detection. And this low temperature. Makes metal as brittle as glass. And the thing may have been crystallized by the vibration."

The plane was coming down in a shallow glide. I looked out at the grim expanse of black ice-crags and glistening snow below us, and it was far from a comforting prospect. But I had a huge amount of confidence in Ray

Summers. I have known him since the day he appeared, from his father's great Arizona ranch, to be a freshman in the School of Mines at El Paso, where I was then an instructor in geology. We have knocked about queer corners of the world together for a good many years. But he is still but a great boy, with the bluff, simple manners of the West.

"Do you think we can land?" I asked.

"Looks like we've got to," he said, grimly.

"And what after that?"

"How should I know? We have the sledge, tent, furs. Food, and fuel for the primus to last a week. There's the rifle, but it must be a thousand miles to anything to shoot. We can do our best."

"We should have had an extra prop."

"Of course. But it was so many pounds, when every pound counted. And who knew the thing would break?"

"We'll never get out on a week's provisions."

"Not a shot! Too bad to disappoint Captain Harper." Ray grinned wanly. "He ought to have the *Albatross* around there by this time, waiting for us." The *Albatross* was the ship which had left us at Little America a few months before, to steam around and pick us up at our destination beyond Enderby Land. "We're in the same boat with Major Meriden and his wife—and all those others. Lost without a trace."

"You've read Scott's diary—that he wrote after he visited the pole in 1912—the one they found with the bodies?"

"Yes. Not altogether cheerful. But we won't be trying to get out. No use of that." He looked at me suddenly, grinning again. "Say, Jim, why not try for that shining mountain we saw? It looks queer enough to be interesting. We ought to make it in a week."

"I'm with you," I said.

I did not speak again, for the jagged ice-peaks were coming rather near. I held my breath as the little plane veered around a slender black spire and dropped toward a tiny scrap of smooth snow among the ice-hummocks. I might have spared my anxiety. Under Ray's consumately skilful piloting, the skids struck the snow with hardly a shock. We glided swiftly over the ice and came to rest just short of a yawning crevasse.

"Suppose," said Ray, "that we spend the first night in the plane. We are tired already. We can keep warm here, and sleep. We've plenty of ice to melt for water. Then we're off for the shining mountain."

I agreed: Ray Summers is usually right. We got out the sledge, packed it, took our bearings, and made all preparations for a start to the luminous mountain, which was about a hundred miles away. The thermometer stood at twenty below, but we were comfortable enough in our furs as we ate a scanty supper and went to sleep in the cabin of the plane.

We started promptly the next morning, after draining the last of the hot chocolate from our vacuum bottles, which we left behind. We had a light but powerful sporting rifle, with telescopic sights, and several hundred rounds of ammunition. Ray put them in the pack, though I insisted that we would never need them, unless a quick way out of our predicament.

"No, Jim," he said. "We take 'em along. We don't know what we're going to find at the shining mountain."

The air was bitterly cold as we set out: it was twenty-five below and a sharp wind was blowing. Only our toiling at the sledge kept us warm. We covered eighteen miles that day, and made a good camp in the lee of a bare stone ridge.

That night there was a slight fall of snow. When we went on it was nearly thirty-five degrees below zero. The layer of fresh snow concealed irregularities in the ice, making our pulling very hard. After an exhausting day we had made hardly fifteen miles.

On the following day the sky was covered with gray clouds, and a bitterly cold wind blew. We should have remained in the tent, but the shortage of food made it imperative that we keep moving. We felt immensely better after a reckless, generous fill of hot pemmican stew; but the next morning my feet were so painful from frost-bite that I could hardly get on my fur boots.

Walking was very painful to me that day, but we made a good distance, having come to smoother ice. Ray was very kind in caring for me. I became discouraged about going on at all: it was very painful, and I knew there was no hope of getting out. I tried to get some of our morphine tablets, but Ray had them, and refused to be convinced that he ought to go on without me.

On the next march we came in sight of the luminous mountain, which cheered me considerably. It was a curious thing, indeed. A straight-sided cone of light it was, rather steeper than the average volcano. Its point was sharp, its sides smooth as if cut with a mammoth plane. And it shone with a pure white light, with a steady and unchanging milky radiance. It rose out of the black and dull yellow of the ice wilderness like a white finger of hope.

The next morning it was a little warmer. Ray had been caring for my feet very attentively, but it took me nearly two hours to get on my footgear. Again I tried to get him to leave me, but he refused.

We arrived at the base of the shining mountain in three more marches. On the last night the fuel for the primus was all gone, having been used up during the very cold weather, and we were unable to melt water to drink. We munched the last of our pemmican dry.

A few minutes after we had started on the last morning, Ray stopped suddenly.

"Look at that!" he cried.

I saw what he had seen—the wreck of an airplane, the wings crumpled up and blackened with fire. We limped up to it.

"A Harley biplane!" Ray exclaimed. "That is Major Meriden's ship! And look at that wing! It looks like it's been in an electric furnace!"

I examined the metal wing; saw that it had been blackened with heat. The metal was fused and twisted.

"I've seen a good many wrecks, Jim. I've seen planes that burned as they fell. But nothing like that. The fuselage and engines were not even afire. Jim, something struck out from that shining mountain and brought them down!"

"Are they—" I began.

Ray was poking about in the snow in the cockpits.

"No. Not here. Probably would have been better for them if they had been killed in the plane. Quick and merciful."

He examined the engines and propellers.

"No. Seems to be nothing wrong. Something struck them down!"

Soon we went on.

The shining mountain rose before us like a great cone of fire. It must have been three thousand feet high, and about that in diameter at the bottom. Its walls were as smooth and straight as though turned from milky rock crystal in a gigantic lathe. It shone with a steady, brilliantly white radiance.

"That's no natural hill!" Ray grunted beside me as we limped on.

We were less than a mile from the foot of the cone of fire. Soon we observed another remarkable thing about it. It seemed that a straight band of silvery metal rose from the snow about its foot.

"Has it a wall around it?" I exclaimed.

"Evidently," said Ray. "Looks as if it's built on a round metal platform. But by whom? When? Why?"

We approached the curious wall. It was of a white metal, apparently aluminum, or a silvery alloy of that metal. In places it was twenty-five feet high, but more usually the snow and ice was banked high against it. The smooth white wall of the gleaming mountain stood several hundred yards back from the wall.

"Let's have a look over it." Ray suggested. "We can get up on that hummock, against it. You know, this place must have been built by men!"

We clambered up over the ice, as he suggested, until our heads came above the top of the wall.

"A lake of fire!" cried Ray.

Indeed, a lake of liquid fire lay before us. The white aluminum wall was hardly a foot thick. It formed a great circular tank, nearly a mile across, with the cone of white fire rising in the center. And the tank was filled, to within a foot of the top, with shimmeringly brilliant white fluid, bright and luminous as the cone—liquid light!

Ray dipped a hand into it. The hand came up with fingers of fire, radiant, gleaming, with shining drops falling from them. With a spasmodic effort, he flung off the luminous drops, rubbed his hand on his garments, and got it back into its fur mitten.

"Gee, it's cold!" he muttered. "Freeze the horns off a brass billy-goat!"

"Cold light!" I exclaimed. "What wouldn't a bottle of that stuff be worth to a chemist back in the States!"

"That cone must be a factory to make the stuff." Ray suggested, hugging his hand. "They might pump the liquid up to the top, and then let it trickle down over the sides: that would explain why the cone is so bright. The stuff might absorb sunlight, like barium sulphide. And there could be chemical action with the air, under the actinic rays."

"Well, if somebody's making cold light, where does he use it?"

"I'd like to find out, and strike him for a hot meal," Ray said, grinning. "It's too cold to live on top of the ground around here. They must run it down in a cave."

"Then let's find the hole."

"You know it's possible we won't be welcome. This mountain of light may be connected with the vanishing of all the aviators. We'd better take along the rifle."

We set off around just outside the white metal wall. The snow and ice was irregularly banked against it, but the wall itself was smooth and unbroken. We had limped along for some two miles, or more than halfway around the amazing lake of light. I had begun to doubt that we would find anything.

Then we came to a square metal tower, ten feet on a side, that rose just outside the silvery wall, to a level with its top. The ice was low here; the tower rose twenty feet above its unequal surface. We found metal flanges riveted to its side, like the steps of a ladder. They were most inconveniently placed, nearly four feet apart; but we were able to climb them, and to look down the shaft.

It was a straight-sided pit, evidently some hundreds of feet deep. We could see a tiny square of light at the bottom, very far away. The flanges ran down the side forming the rungs of a ladder that gave access to whatever lay at the bottom.

Without hesitation, Ray climbed over the side and started down. I followed him, feeling a great relief in getting out of the freezing wind. Ray had the rifle and ammunition strapped to his back, along with a few other articles; and I had a small pack. We had abandoned the sledge, with the useless stove and the most of our instruments. Our food was all gone.

The metal flanges were fully four feet apart, and it was not easy to scramble down from one to another; certainly not easy for one who was cold, hungry, thirsty, worn out with a week of exhausting marches, and suffering the torture of frozen feet.

"You know, this thing was not built by men," Ray observed.

"Not built by men? What do you mean?"

"Men would have put the steps closer together. Jim, I'm afraid we are up against something—well—that we aren't used to."

"If men didn't build this, what did?" I was astounded.

"Search me! This continent has been cut off from the rest of the world for geologic ages. Such life as has been found here is not common to the rest of the earth. It is not impossible that some form of life, isolated here, has developed intelligence and acquired the power to erect that cone of light—and to burn the wing off a metal airplane."

My thoughts whirled madly as we clambered down the shaft.

It must have taken us an hour to reach the bottom. I did not count the steps, but it must have been at least a thousand feet. The air grew rapidly warmer as we descended. We both took off most of our heavy fur garments, and left them hanging on the rungs.

I was rather nervous. I felt the nearness of an intelligent, hostile power. I had a great fear that the owners of those steps would use them to find us, and then crush us ruthlessly as they had brought down Meriden's plane.

The little square of white light below grew larger. Finally I saw Ray swing off and stand on his feet in a flood of white radiance below me. The air was warm, moist, laden with a subtle unfamiliar fragrance that suggested growing things. Then I stood beside Ray.

We stood on the bare stone floor of a huge cavern. It must have been of volcanic origin. The walls glistened with the sparkling smoothness of volcanic glass. It was a huge space. The black roof was a hundred feet high, or more; the cave was some hundreds of feet wide. And it sloped away from us into dim distance as though leading into huger cavities below.

The light that shone upon us came from an amazing thing—a fall of liquid fire. From the roof plunged a sheer torrent of white brilliantly luminous fluid, falling a hundred feet into a shimmering pool of moon-flame. Shining opalescent mists swirled about it, and the ceaseless roar of it filled the cave with sound. It seemed that a stream of the phosphorescent stuff ran off down the cave from the pool, to light the lower caverns.

"Very clever!" said Ray. "They make the stuff up there at the cone and run it in here to see by."

"This warm air feels mighty good," I remarked, pulling off another garment.

Ray sniffed the air. "A curious odor. Smells like something growing. Where anything is growing there ought to be something to eat. Let's see what we can find."

Only black obsidian covered the floor about us. Cautiously we skirted the overflowing pool of white fire, and followed down the stream of it that flowed toward the inner cavern. We had gone but a few hundred yards when suddenly Ray stopped me with a hand on my arm.

"Lie flat!" he hissed. "Quick!"

He dived behind a huge mass of fire-born granite. I flung myself down beside him.

"Something is coming up the trail by the shining river. And it isn't a man! It's between us and the light; we should be able to see it."

Soon I heard a curious scraping sound, and a little tinkle of metal. I caught a whiff of a powerful odor—a strange, fishy odor—so strong that it almost knocked me down.

The thing that made the scraping and the tinkle and the smell came into view. The sight of it sickened me with horror.

It was far larger than a man; its body was heavy as a horse's, but nearer the ground. In form it suggested a huge crab, though it was not very much like any crustacean I had ever seen. It was mostly red in color, and covered with a huge scarlet shell. It had five pairs of limbs. The two forward pairs had pinchers, seemingly used as hands; it scraped along on the other three pairs. Yard-long antennae, slender and luminously green, wavered above a grotesque head. The many facets of compound eyes stood on the end of foot-long stalks.

The amazing crab-thing wore a metal harness. Bands of silvery aluminum were fastened about its shell, with little cases of white metal dangling to them. In one of its uplifted claws it carried what seemed to be an aluminum bar, two feet long and an inch thick.

It scraped lumberingly past, between us and the racing stream of white fire. It passed less than a dozen feet from us. The curious fishy smell of it was overpowering, disgusting.

Sweat of horror chilled my limbs. The monster emanated power, sinister, malevolent power, power intelligent, alien and hostile to man.

I trembled with the fear that it would see us, but it scrambled grotesquely on. When it was twenty yards past, Ray picked up a block of black lava that lay beneath his hand and hurled it silently and swiftly. It crashed splinteringly on the rocks far beyond the creature, on the other side of the stream of light.

In fascination I watched the monster as it paused as if astonished. The glittering compound eyes twisted about on their stalks, and the long shining green tentacles wavered questioningly. Then the knobbed limbs snapped the white metal tube to a level position. A metallic click came from it.

And a ray of red light, vivid and intense, burst from the tube. It flashed across the river of fire. With a dull, thudding burst it struck the rocks where the stone had fallen. It must have been a ray of concentrated heat. Rocks beneath it flashed into sudden incandescence, splintered and cracked, flowed in molten streams.

In a moment the intensely brilliant ruby ray flashed off. The rocks in the circle where it had struck faded to a dull red and then to blackness, still cracking and crumbling.

To my intense relief, the monstrous crab lumbered on.

"That," Ray whispered, "is what got Major Meriden's airplane wing."

When we could hear its scraping progress no longer, we climbed up from behind our boulder and continued cautiously down the cavern, beside the rushing luminous river. In half a mile we came to a bend. Rounding it, we gazed upon a remarkable sight.

We looked into a huge cavity in the heart of the earth. A vast underground plain lay before us, with the black lava of the roof arching above it. It must have been miles across, though we had no way to measure it, and it stretched down into dim hazy distance. Its level was hundreds of feet below us.

At our feet the glistening river of fire plunged down again in a magnificent flaming fall. Below, its luminous liquid was spread out in rivers and lakes and canals, over all the vast plain. The channels ran through an amazing jungle. It was a forest of fungus, of mushroom things with great fleshy stalks and spreading circular tops. But they were not the sickly white and yellow of ordinary mushrooms, but were of brilliant colors, bright green, flaming scarlet, gold and purple-blue. Huge brilliant yellow stalks, fringed with crimson and black, lifted mauve tops thirty feet or more. It was a veritable forest of flame-bright fungus.

In the center of this weirdly forested subterranean plain was a great lake, filled, not with the flaming liquid, but with dark crystal water. And on the bottom of that lake, clearly visible from the elevation upon which we stood, was a city!

A city below the water! The buildings were upright cylinders in groups of two or three, of dozens, even of hundreds. For miles, the bottom of the great lake was covered with them. They were all of crystal, azure-blue, brilliant as cylinders turned from immense sapphires. They were vividly visible beneath the transparent water. Not one of them broke the surface.

Through the clear black water we saw moving hundreds, thousands of the giant crabs. The crawled over the hard, pebbled bottom of the lake, or swam between the crystal cylinders of the city. They were huge as the one we had seen, with red shells, great ominous looking stalked eyes, luminous green tentacular antennae and knobbed claws on forelimbs.

"Looks as if we've run on something to write home about," Ray muttered in amazement.

"A whole city of them! A whole world! No wonder they could build that cone-mountain for a lighting plant!"

"When they got to knocking down airplanes with that heat-ray," he speculated, "they were probably surprised to find that other animals had developed intelligence."

"Do you suppose those mushroom things are good to eat?"

"We can try and see—if the crabs don't get us first with a heat-ray. I'm hungry enough to try anything!"

Again we cautiously advanced. The river of light fell over a sheer precipice, but we found a metal ladder spiked to the rock, with rungs as inconveniently far apart as those in the shaft. It was five hundred feet, I suppose, to the bottom; it took us many minutes to descend.

At last we stepped off in a little rocky clearing. The forest of brilliant mushrooms rose about us, great fleshy stalks of gold and graceful fringes of black and scarlet about them, with flattened heads of purple.

We started eagerly across toward the fungoid forest. I had visions of tearing off great pieces of soft, golden flesh and filling my aching stomach with it.

We were stopped by a sharp, poignantly eager human cry.

A human being, a girl, darted from among the mushroom stalks and ran across to us. Sobbing out great incoherent cries, she dropped at Ray's feet, wrapped her arms about his knees and clung to him, while her slender body was wracked with sobbing cries.

My first impression was that she was very beautiful—and that impression I was never called upon to revise. About her lithe young body she had the merest scrap of some curious green fabric—ample in the warm air of the great cavern. Luxuriant brown hair fell loose about her white shoulders. She was not quite twenty years old, I supposed; her body was superbly formed, with the graceful curves and the free, smooth movements of a wild thing.

Ray stood motionless for a moment, thunder-struck as I was, while the sobbing girl clung to his knees. Then the astonishment on his face gave place to pity.

"Poor kid!" he murmured.

He bent, took her tenderly by the shoulder, helped her to her feet.

Her beauty burst upon us like a great light. Smoothly white, her skin was, perfect. Wide blue eyes, now appealing, even piteous, looked from beneath a wealth of golden brown hair. White teeth, straight and even, flashed behind the natural crimson of her lips.

She stood staring at Ray, in a sort of enchantment of wonder. An eager light of incredible joy flamed in her amazing eyes; red lips were parted in an unconscious smile of joy. She looked like the troubled princess in the fairy tale, when the prince of her dreams appeared in the flesh.

"God, but you're beautiful!" Ray's words slipped out as if he were hardly conscious of them. He flushed quickly, stepped back a little.

The girl's lips opened. She voiced a curious cry. It was deep toned, pealing with a wonderful timbre. A happy burst of sound, like a baby makes. But strong, ringing, musically golden. And pathetically eager, pitifully glad, so that it brought tears to my eyes, cynical old man that I am.

I saw Ray wipe his eyes.

"Can you talk?" Ray put the question in a clear, deliberate voice, with great kindness ringing in it.

"Talk?" The chiming, golden voice was slow, uncertain. "Talk? Yes. I talked—with mother. But for long—I have had no need to talk."

"Where is your mother?" Ray's voice was gentle.

"She is gone. She was here when I was little." The clear, silvery voice was more certain now. "Once, when I was almost as big as she—she was still. She was cold. She did not move when I called her. The Things took her away. She was dead. She told me that sometime she would be dead."

Bright tears came in the wide blue eyes, trickled down over the perfect face. A pathetic catch was in the deliberate, halting voice. I turned away, and Ray put a handkerchief to his face.

"What is your name? Who are you?" Ray spoke kindly.

"I am Mildred. Mildred Meriden."

"Meriden!" Ray turned to me. "I bet this is a daughter of the major and his wife!"

"Father was the major," the girl said slowly. "He and mother came in a machine that flew, from a far land. The Things burned the machine with the red fire. They came here and the Things kept them. They made mother sing over the water. They killed father. I never saw him."

"I know," Ray, said gently. "We came from the same land. We saw your father's machine above."

"You came from outside! And you are going back? Oh, take me with you! Take me!" Piteous pleading was in her voice. "It is so—lonely since the Things took Mother away. Mother told me that sometime men would come, and take me away to see the people and the outside that she told me of. Oh, please take me!"

"Don't worry! You go along whenever we leave—if we can get out."

"Oh, I am so glad! You are very good!"

Impulsively, she threw her arms around Ray's neck. Gently, he disengaged himself, flushing a little. I noticed, however, that he did not seem particularly displeased.

"But can we get out?"

"Mother and I tried. We could never get out. The Things watch. They make me come to the water to sing, when the great bell rings."

"Are these things goods to eat?" I motioned to the brilliant fungal forest. I had begun to fear that Ray would never get to this very important topic.

Blue eyes regarded me. "Eat? Oh, you are hungry! Come! I have food."

Like a child, she grasped Ray's hand, pulled him toward the mushroom jungle. I followed, and we slipped in between the brilliantly golden, fleshy stalks. They rose to the tangle of bright feathery fringes above, huge and substantial as the trunks of trees.

In a few minutes we came to a wide, shallow canal, metal-walled, through which a slow current of the opalescent, luminous liquid was flowing. We crossed this on a narrow metal foot-bridge, and went on through the brilliant forest.

Suddenly we emerged into a little clearing, with the black waters of the great lake visible beyond it, across a quarter-mile of rocky beach. In the middle of the open space, rose three straight cylinders of azure crystal, side by side. Each must have been twenty feet in diameter, and forty high. They shone with a clear blue light, like the cylindrical buildings we had seen in the strange city of the crab-creatures below the great lake.

Mildred Meriden, the strangely beautiful girl who had known no other world than this amazing cavern empire where giant crabs reigned, beckoned us with unconscious queenly grace to enter the arched door in the blue sapphire wall of her remarkable abode of clustered cylinders.

The crystal of the walls seemed luminous, the lofty cylinders were filled with a liquid, azure radiance. The high round room we entered was strangely furnished. There was a silken couch, a bathing pool of blue crystal filled with sparkling water, a curious chest of drawers made of bright aluminum with a mirror of polished crystal, its top bearing odd combs and other articles. The furnishings must have been done by the giant crabs, under human direction.

Mildred led us quickly across the room, through an arched opening into another. A round aluminum table stood in the center of the room, with two curious metal chairs beside it. Odd metal cabinets stood about the shining blue walls. The girl made us sit down, and put dishes before us.

She gave us each a bowl of thick, sweetish soup, darkly red; placed before us a dish piled high with little circular cakes, crisp and brown, which had a tantalizing fragrance; poured for each of us a transparent crystal goblet full of clear amber drink.

We fell to with enthusiasm and abandon.

"The Things made this place for father," the girl told us, as she watched us eat, attentively replenishing the red soup in the great blue crystal bowl, or the little cakes, or the fragrant amber drink. "They would give him anything he wanted. But he tried to go away with mother, and they killed him."

"We must get out of here," Ray declared when at last we had done. "We must get together a lot of food, and enough clothing for all of us. We ought to be able to make it to the edge of the ice-pack. We've got to give these crab-things the slip; we ought to get off before they know we're here—unless they already do."

Mildred was eagerly attentive: she was so unused to human speech that it took the best of her efforts to understand us, though it seems that her mother had given her quite a wide education. She promised that there would be no difficulty about the food.

"Mother taught me how to fix food," she said. "She always said that sometime men would come, with weapons of fire and great noise that would tear and kill the Things. I have food ready, in bags—more than we can carry. I have, too, the furs that mother and father wore."

She ran into another room and returned with a great pile of fur garments, which we examined and found to be in good condition.

"Now is the time," Ray said. "I'd like to know more about the big crabs, but there'll be a chance for that, later. Mildred is the important thing, now. We must get her out. Then we can tell the world about this place and come back with a bigger expedition."

"You think we can reach the coast?"

"I think so. It might be hard on Mildred. But we will have food; we can probably find fuel for the stove in Meriden's plane, if the tanks were well sealed. And Captain Harper should have a relief party landed and sent to meet us. We should have only three or four hundred miles to go alone."

"Three or four hundred miles, over country like we've been crossing in the last week, with a girl! Ray, we'd never make it!"

"It's the only chance."

I said nothing more. I knew that I could stand no such march on my frozen feet, but I resolved to say nothing about it. I would help them as far as I could, and then walk out of camp some night. Men have done just that.

Mildred brought out sacks of the little cakes, and of a red powder that seemed to be the dried and ground flesh of a crimson mushroom. We made a pack for each of us, as heavy as we could carry.

Just before we were ready to start Ray took off my footgear and treated my feet from his medicine kit. I had feared gangrene, but he assured me that there was no danger if they were well cared for. Walking was still exquisitely painful to me as we slipped out through the arched door and into the fungoid forest beyond the three blue cylinders.

As rapidly and silently as possible we hastened through the brilliant fungous forest, across the river of opalescent liquid, to the foot of the fall of fire. A weird and splendid sight was that sheer arc of shimmering white flame, roaring into a pool of opal light, and surrounded with a mist of moon-flame.

We reached the foot of the metal ladder spiked to the rocks beside the fall and started up immediately. The going was not easy. The packs of food, heavy enough when we were on level ground, were difficult indeed to lift when one was scrambling up over rungs four feet apart.

Ray climbed ahead, with a piece of rope fastened from his waist to Mildred's, so that he could help her if she slipped. I was below the girl. We were halfway up the rock when suddenly a glare of red light shone upon me, casting my shadow sharply on the cliff. I looked up and saw the broad, intensely red beam of a heat-ray like that we had seen the giant crab use.

The ray came, evidently, from the shore of the great lake with its submerged city of blue cylinders. It fell upon the face of the cliff just above us. Quickly the ladder was heated to cherry red. The face of the rock grew incandescent, cracked. Hot sparks rained down upon us.

Slowly the ray moved down, toward us.

"Guess we'd better call it off," said Ray. "They have the advantage right now. Better get to climbing down, Jim. This ladder is going to be burning my hands pretty soon."

I climbed down. Mildred and Ray scrambled down behind me.

The ray followed us, keeping the metal at a cherry red just above Ray's hands.

I looked down and saw a dozen of the giant crabs lumbering up out of the fungoid jungle from the direction of the great lake. Hideous things they were, with staring, stalked eyes, shining green antennae, polished red shells, claw-armed limbs. Like the one that had passed us in the upper cavern, they wore glistening white metal accoutrements.

We clambered down, with the red ray following.

I dropped to the ground among them, wet with the sweat of horror. I reeled in nausea from the intolerable odor of the crab-things; it was indescribable, overpowering.

Curious rasping stridulations came from them, sounds which seemed to serve as means of communication, and which Mildred evidently understood.

"They say that you will not be harmed, but that you must not go out," she called down.

I was seized by the pincher-like claws, held writhing in an unbreakable grasp, while the glittering eyes twisted about, looked at me, and the shining green tentacles wavered questioningly over me. My stomach revolted at the horrible odor.

The crabs tore off my pack, even my clothing. Ray was similarly treated as soon as he reached the ground. Though they took Mildred's pack, they treated her with a curious respect.

In a few minutes they released us. They had taken the packs, the rifle and ammunition, our medicine kit and the few instruments we had brought with us down the shaft, even our clothing. They turned us loose stark naked. Ray's face and neck went beet-red when he saw Mildred standing by him.

The rasping sound came from one of them again.

"It says you may stay with me," Mildred said. "They will not harm you unless you try again to get away. If you do, you die—as father did. They will keep what they took from you."

Several of the creatures went scraping off, carrying the articles they had taken from us either in their claws or in the metal cases they wore. Several waited, staring at us with the stalked compound eyes, and waving the green antennae as if they were organs of some special sense.

Two of the creatures waited at the foot of the metal ladder, holding the long slender white tubes of the heat-ray in their claws.

"They say we can go now," Mildred said.

She led the way toward the edge of the brilliant jungle. She seemed to be without false modesty, for I saw her glancing with evident admiration at Ray's lithe and powerful white-skinned figure. We followed her into the giant mushrooms, glad to escape the overpowering stench of the crabs.

In a few minutes we arrived again at the strange building of the three blue cylinders. Mildred, noticing our discomfort, produced for each of us a piece of white silken fabric with which we draped ourselves.

She had noticed my difficulty in walking on bare feet. She had me bathe them, then dressed them with a soothing yellow oil, and bandaged them skilfully.

"Anyhow," she said later, "it is good to have both of you here with me. I am sorry indeed for you that you may never see your country again. But it is good fortune for me. I was so lonely."

"These damned crabs don't know me!" Ray Summers muttered. "They think I'll play around like a pet kitten, for the rest of my life! They'll get their eyes opened. We'll spend the winter on Palm Beach yet!"

"It seems to me that we're rather outnumbered." I said. "And it's rather more pleasant in here than outside."

"I'm going to get that rifle," Ray declared, "and give these big crabs a little respect for humanity!"

"Let's rest up a while first, anyhow," I urged.

Presently Mildred noticed how tired we were. She went into the third of the connected cylinders of blue crystal, was busy a few minutes and called us to the couches she had prepared there.

"You may sleep," she told us. "The Things never come here. And they said they would not harm you, if you did not try to go out."

We lay down on the silken beds. In a few minutes I was sleep. I awoke to feel a curious unease, a sense of impending catastrophe. Ray was bending over me, his face drawn with anxiety.

"Something's happened!" he whispered. "She's gone!"

I sat up, staring into the liquid blue vastness of the tall cylinder above us.

"Listen! What's that?"

A deep bell-note sounded out, brazen, clanging. Sonorous, throbbing, mighty, it rang through the cylindered rooms. Slowly it died; faded to silence with a last ringing pulse. Tense minutes of silence passed. Again it boomed out, throbbed, and died. After more long minutes there was yet a third.

"Outside, somewhere!"

Ray started; ran to the arched door. We looked out upon the dense forest of gold and crimson mushrooms that grew below the black cavern roof. Before us, across a few hundred yards of bare rocky beach, was the edge of the crystal lake with the city of blue cylinders upon its floor.

"God! What's that?" Ray gripped my arm crushingly.

A thin wailing scream came across the beach from the black lake. A piteous sound it was, plaintive, pleading. Higher and higher it rose, until it was a piercing silver note. Clear and sweet it was, but inexpressibly lonely, sorrowful, mournful. It sank slowly, died away. Again it rose and fell, and again.

"It's Mildred!" I gasped. "Didn't she say something about singing to the crabs?"

"Yes! I think she did. Well, if that's singing, it's wonderful! Had me feeling like I'd never see another human. But listen—"

Liquid, trilling notes were rising, pealing out in a queer, swift rhythm. It was happy, joyous, carefree. The rippling golden tones made me think of the caroling of birds on a spring morning. Swiftly it rose and fell, pure and clear as the tinkle of a mountain brook.

Mildred sang not words but notes of pure music.

The gay song died.

And the strong clear voice rose again with the force and challenge of bugle notes, with a swift marching time beating through it. It throbbed to a rhythm strange to me. It set my feet tingling to move; it set my heart to pulsing faster. It was a challenge to action, to battle.

Unconsciously obeying the suggestion of the song, Ray whispered, "Let's get over and see what's going on."

We leaped through the door and ran across four hundred yards of rocky beach to the edge of the lake. We stepped on a granite bluff a few yards above the water, to gaze upon as strange a sight as men ever saw.

The black water lay before us, a transparent crystal sheet. On its rocky bottom we could see the innumerable clusters of upright azure cylinders that were the city of the crabs. The blue cylinders seemed to bend and waver in the water.

A hundred yards away from us, over the dark water, was Mildred. She stood on a slender azure cylinder that came just to the surface. Tall, slender, superbly graceful, with only the scant bodice of green silken stuff about her, she looked like the statue of a goddess in white marble. Her head was thrown up, golden-brown hair fell behind her shoulders, and the pure notes of her song rang over the water.

Beyond her, all about her, were thousands upon thousands of the giant crabs, swimming at the surface of the water. Their green antenna rose above the water, a curious forest of luminous tentacles, flexing, wavering. Green coils moved and swung in time to the strange rhythm of her song.

The last note died. Her white arms fell in a gesture of finality. The thousands of twisting green antennae vanished below the water, and the giant red crabs swam swiftly back to the tall blue cylinders of their submerged city.

The white goddess turned and saw us.

Her voice rang out in a golden shout of welcome. With a clean dive she slipped into the water and came swimming swiftly toward us. Her slim white body glided through the crystal water as smoothly as a fish. Reaching the shore she sprang to her feet and ran to meet Ray.

"The Things come together when the giant bell rings, to listen to my song," she said. "They like my singing, as they liked mother's. But for that, they would not let us live. That is the reason they would not let us go."

"I like your singing, too," Ray informed her. "Though at first you made me cry. It was so lonely."

"The song was lonely because I have been lonely. Did you hear the glad song I sang because you have come?"

"Sure! Great stuff! Made me feel like a kid at Christmas!"

"Come," she said. "We will eat."

Like a child, she took Ray's hand again, smiling naively up at him as she led the way toward the three sapphire cylinders.

Back in the blue-vaulted dining room, Ray made Mildred sit with me at the little metal table while he served the little brown cakes and the dark-red soup and the fragrant amber drink. Mildred got up and brought a great metal bowl filled with tiny purple fruits that had a delicious, piquant tang.

Ray was deeply thoughtful as he ate. Suddenly he sat back and cried out:

"I've got it!"

"Got what?" I demanded.

"I want that rifle! Mildred can find out where it is. Then, when she sings, the crabs will all come. I'll get the gun, while she is singing, and hide it. Then when it comes time to get out, she will sing while you and I are getting our packs up the cliff. I can cover them with the rifle while she gets up to us."

"Looks good enough," I agreed, "provided they all come to hear the singing."

He explained the plan at greater length to the girl. She assured him that the crabs all come when the bell-notes sound. She thought that she could make them return her furs, and find out where they had put the gun.

My feet were much better than they had been, and Mildred dressed them again with the yellow oil. Ray examined them, said that I should be able to walk as well as ever in a few days.

Considerable time went by. Since the crabs had taken our watches, we had no very accurate way of counting days; but I think we slept about a dozen times. Ray and Mildred spent a good deal of time together, and seemed not altogether to hate each other. By the end of the time my feet were quite well; I did not even lose a toe.

We went over our plans for escape in great detail. The crabs had confiscated our clothing. Mildred managed to secure the return of her furs, and, incidentally, while she was about it, learned where the rifle was.

Fortunately, perhaps realizing that it would be ruined by water, the crabs had not taken it to their submerged city. Being amphibious, they lived above water as easily as below, and much of their industrial equipment was above the surface. The great pumps which lifted the white phosphorescent liquid from the canals back to the cone above the ground were located beyond the great lake. I did not see the place, but Ray tells me that they had great engines and a wealth of strange and complex machinery there. It was at these pumps that they had left our rifle and instruments, as Mildred found when she was recovering her furs.

They had taken our food, and we prepared as much more as we could carry, arranged sacks for it, and made quilted garments for ourselves.

Then the three brazen notes clanged out, and Mildred ran across the beach and swam out to the blue cylinder to sing. Ray slipped hurriedly away, while the green forest of antennae was still growing up from the water about the girl.

I waited above the beach, enchanted by the haunting, wordless melody of the gongs. It seemed that only a few minutes had passed, though it may have been an hour or more, when Ray was by my side again. He flourished the rifle.

"I've got it! In good shape, too. Hasn't even been fired, though it looks like they have opened a box of cartridges, and cut open one or two. Maybe they didn't understand the outfit—or it may be such a primitive weapon that they aren't interested in it."

We hurried up to the building of blue cylinders and carefully hid the gun and ammunition, as well as a sun compass, a pair of prism binoculars, and a few other articles Ray had recovered.

In a few minutes Mildred, having seen Ray's return, finished her song and ran up to join us. We arranged our packs, and waited the next call of the throbbing brazen gong to make the attempt for freedom.

We slept twice again before the clang of the great gong. Ray and Mildred were always together; I could not see that they were at all impatient.

The bell note came, the awful brazen vibration of it ringing on the black cavern roof. It came when we were eating, in the liquid turquoise radiance of the lofty cylinder. We sprang out. Ray gave his last directions to Mildred.

"Give us time to get to the top of the cliff by the shining fall. Then swim ashore and run. They may not notice. And if they do, we give 'em a taste of lead!"

I was not very much surprised when he took the girl in his arms and put a burning kiss on her red lips. She gasped, but her struggles subsided very quickly; she clung to him as he freed her.

She paused a moment in the door, before she ran down across the beach. A radiant light of joy was burning in her great blue eyes, even though tears were glistening there.

Ray and I waited, to give time for the giant crabs that guarded the ladder to get away. In about ten more minutes the second brazen gong sounded, and presently the third. We gathered up the heavy packs of food. Ray took the rifle and I the binoculars, and we slipped out into the brilliant mushroom forest.

I stepped confidently out of the jungle into the clearing below the splendid opalescent fall of fire—and threw myself backward in trembling panic. A flaming crimson ray cut hissing into the towering mushrooms above my head.

Mildred's confidence that the crabs would all gather at the ringing of the gong had been mistaken. The two guards had been waiting at the foot of the ladder, their flaming heat-rays ready for use.

As I dived back into the jungle, I heard two quick reports of the rifle. I scrambled awkwardly to my feet, beneath the heavy pack. Ray stood alert beside me, the smoking rifle in his hand. The giant crabs had collapsed by the foot of the ladder, in grotesque and hideous metal-bound heaps of red shell and twisted limb. Blood was oozing from a ragged hole in the head of each.

"Glad they were here," Ray muttered. "I wanted to try the gun out on 'em. They're soft enough beneath the shell; the bullet tears 'em up inside. Let's get a move on!"

He sprang past the revolting carcasses. I followed, holding my nose against their nauseating, charnel-house odor. We scrambled up the metal ladder.

As we climbed, I could hear the haunting melody of Mildred's wordless song coming faint across the distance. Once I glanced back for a moment, and glimpsed her tiny white figure above the black water, with the thousands of green antennae rising in a luminous forest about her.

We reached the top of the cliff, where the opalescent river plunged down in the flaming fall. Ray chose convenient boulders for shelter and quickly we flung ourselves flat. Ray replaced the fired cartridges in the rifle and leveled it across the rock before him. I unslung the binoculars and focussed them.

"Watch 'em close," Ray muttered. "And tell me when to shoot."

The black lake lay below us, with the weird city of sapphire cylinders on its floor. I got the glasses upon Mildred's white form. Soon she dived from the turquoise pedestal, swam swiftly ashore and vanished in the vivid fungous jungle. The wavering green antennae vanished below the water; I watched the crabs swimming away. Some of them climbed out of the water and lumbered off in various directions.

In fifteen minutes the slender white form of Mildred appeared at the foot of the ladder. She sprang over the dead crabs and scrambled nimbly up. Soon she was halfway up the face of the cliff, and there had been no sign of discovery. My hopes ran high.

I was sweeping the whole plain with the binoculars, while Ray peered through the telescopic sights of the rifle. Suddenly I saw a giant crab pause as he lumbered along the edge of the black lake. He rose upright; his shining green antennae wavered. Then I saw him reaching with a knobbed claw for a slender silver tube slung to his harness.

"Quick! The one by the lake! To the right of that canal!"

I pointed quickly. Ray swung his gun about, aimed. A broad red beam flashed from the tube the thing carried, and fell upon the cliff. The report of Ray's rifle rang thunderously in my ears. The red ray was snapped off abruptly, and the giant crab rolled over into the black water of the lake. Half a dozen of the huge crabs were in sight. They all took alarm, probably having seen the flash of the red ray. They raised grotesque heads, twisted stalked eyes and waved green antennae. Some of them began to raise the metal tubes of the heat-ray.

"Let's get all there are in sight!" Ray muttered.

He began firing regularly, with deliberate precision. A few times he had to take two shots, but ordinarily one was enough to bring down a giant crab in a writhing red mass. Three times a red ray flashed out, once at the girl clambering up the ladder, twice at our position above the precipice. But the intense color of the ray announced its source, and Ray stopped each before it could be focussed to do damage.

I looked over at Mildred and saw that she was still climbing bravely, a little over a hundred feet below.

Then the great red crabs began to climb out of the water, heat-ray tubes grasped in their claws. Ray fired as fast as he could load and aim. Still he shot with deliberate care, and almost every shot was effective.

Intense, ruby-red rays flashed up from the lake shore. Twice, one of them beat scorchingly upon us for a moment. Once a rock beside us was fused and cracked with the heat. But Ray fired rapidly, and the rays winked out as fast as they were born.

He was powder-stained, black and grimy. The heat-ray had singed his clothing. He was dripping perspiration. The gun was so hot that he could hardly handle it. But still the angry bark of the rifle rang out, almost with a deliberate rhythm. Ray was a fine shot in his youth on his father's Arizona ranch, but his best shooting, I think, was done from above that cascade of liquid fire, at the hordes of monster scarlet crabs.

Mildred scrambled over the edge, unharmed. Her breast was heaving, but her face was bright with joy.

"You are wonderful!" she gasped to Ray.

We seized the packs and beat a hurried retreat. A crimson forest of the heat-rays flashed up behind us, and flamed upon the black walls and roof of the cavern until glistening lava became incandescent, cracked and fused.

We were below the line of the rays. Quickly we made the bend in the cavern and followed at a halting run up the path beside the shimmering river of opalescent light. Before us the torrent of fire fell in a magnificent flaming arc from the roof.

We rounded the pool of lambent milk of flame, passed the roaring torrent of coruscating liquid radiance and reached the ladder in the square, metal shaft. "If we can get to the top before they can get up here, we're safe," Ray said. "If we don't, this shaft will be a chimney of fire."

In the haste of desperation, we attacked the thousand-foot climb. I went first, Mildred below me, and Ray, with the rifle, in the rear. Our heavy packs were a terrible impediment, but we dared not attempt to go on without them. The metal rungs were four feet apart; it was no easy task to scramble from one to the next, again and again, for hundreds of times.

It must have taken us an hour to make it. We should have been caught long before we reached the top, but the giant crabs were slow in their lumbering movements. Despite their evident intelligence, they seemed to lack anything like our railways and automobiles.

The cold gray light of the polar sky came about us; a dull, purple-blue square grew larger above. I clambered over the last rung, flung myself across the top of the metal shaft. Looking down at the tiny fleck of white light so far below, I saw a bit of red move in it.

"A crab!" I shouted. "Hurry!"

Mildred was just below me. I took her pack and helped her over the edge.

Red flame flared up the shaft.

We reached over, seized Ray's arms and fairly jerked him out of the ruby ray.

The bitterly cold wind struck our hot, perspiring bodies as we scrambled down the rungs outside the square metal shaft. Mildred shivered in her thin attire.

"Out of the frying pan into the ice box!" Ray jested grimly as we dropped, to the frozen plain.

Quickly we tore open our packs. Ray and I snatched out clothing and wrapped up the trembling girl. In a few minutes we had her snugly dressed in the fur garments that had been Major Meriden's. Then we got into the quilted garments we had made for ourselves.

The intensely red heat-beam still flared up the shaft. Ray looked at it in satisfaction.

"They'll have it so hot they can't get up it for some time yet," he remarked hopefully.

We shouldered our packs and set out over the wilderness of snow, turning our backs upon the metal-bound lake of fire, with the tall cone of iridescent flame rising in its center.

The deep, purple-blue sky was clear, and, for a rarity, there was not much wind. I doubt that the temperature was twenty below. But it was a violent change from the warm cavern. Mildred was blue and shivering.

In two hours the metal rim below the great white cone had vanished behind the black ice-crags. We passed near the wreck of Major Meriden's plane and reached our last camp, where we had left the tent sledge, primus stove, and most of our instruments. The tent was still stretched, though banked with snow. We got Mildred inside, chafed her hands, and soon had her comfortable.

Then Ray went out and soon returned with a sealed tin of oil from the wrecked plane, with which he lit the primus stove. Soon the tent was warm. We melted snow and cooked thick red soup. After the girl had made a meal of the scalding soup, with the little golden cakes, she professed to be feeling as well as ever.

"We can fix our plane!" Ray said. "There's a perfectly good prop on Meriden's plane!"

We went back to the wreck, found the tools, and removed an undamaged propeller. This we packed on the sledge, with a good supply of fuel for the stove.

"I'm sure we're safe now, so far as the crab-things go," he said. "I don't fancy they'd get around very well in the snow."

In an hour we broke camp, and made ten miles of the distance back to the plane before we stopped. We were anxious about Mildred, but she seemed to stand the journey admirably; she is a marvelous physical specimen. She seemed running over with gay vivacity of spirit; she asked innumerable questions of the world which she had known only at second-hand from her mother's words.

The weather smiled on us during the march back to the plane as much as it had frowned on the terrible journey to the cone. We had an abundance of food and fuel, and we made it in eight easy stages. Once there was a light fall of snow, but the air was unusually warm and calm for the season.

We found the plane safe. It was the work of but a short time to remove the broken propeller and replace it with the one we had brought from the wrecked ship. We warmed and started the engine, broke the skids loose from the ice, turned the plane around, and took off safely from the tiny scrap of smooth ice.

Mildred seemed amazed and immensely delighted at the sensations of her first trip aloft.

A few hours later we were landing beside the *Albatross*, in the leaden blue sea beyond the ice barrier. Bluff Captain Harper greeted us in amazed delight as we climbed to the deck.

"You're just in time!" he said. "The relief expedition we landed came back a week ago. We had no idea you could still be alive, with only a week's provisions. We were sailing to-morrow. But tell us! What happened? Your passenger—"

"We just stopped to pick up my fiancee," Ray grinned. "Captain, may I present Miss Mildred Meriden? We'll be wanting you to marry us right away."

THE MENACE OF THE INSECT

It is possible that future study may tell man enough about insects to enable him to eradicate them. This, however, is more than can be reasonably expected, for the more we cultivate the earth the better we make conditions for these enemies. The insect thrives on the work of man. And having made conditions ideal for the insect, with great expanses of cultivated food fitted to his needs, it is an optimist who can believe that at the same time we can make other conditions which will be so unfavorable as to cause him to disappear completely. The two things do not go together.

The insect is much better fitted for life than is man. He can survive long periods of famine, he can survive extremes of heat and cold. The insect produces great numbers of young which have no long period of infancy requiring the attention of the parents over a large part of their life. Every function of the insect is directed toward the propagation of the race and the use of minimum effort in every other direction.

It is even possible in some cases, the water flea, for example, for the female to produce young without the necessity of fertilization by the male. In order to perform the necessary work to insure food supplies for the winter other insects have developed highly specialized workers, especially fitted to do particular kinds of labor. Ants and termites are in this class.

If we examine the organization of insects closely we shall find but one point at which they are vulnerable. This is in their lack of ability to reason. True, there is considerable evidence to support the belief that some insects are capable of simple reasoning, but the development in this direction is only of the most elementary nature. As compared to man it is safe to say that they do not reason. They are guided by instinct.

This again is the most efficient way to organize their affairs. It requires no long period of training. They can begin performing all their useful functions as soon as their bodily development makes it possible. No one need teach them how to catch their prey, how to build their nests or shelters. Instinct takes care of this. But this, obviously the best system in a world wholly governed by instinct, is not so desirable when the instinctively actuated insect encounters another form of life, as man, which is capable of reason. The reasoning individual can play all kinds of tricks on the individual who is actuated by instinct.

My whole attention was focused upon the strange beings.

THE GHOST WORLD

By Sewell Peaslee Wright

Commander John Hanson records another of his thrilling interplanetary adventures with the Special Patrol Service.

I was asleep when our danger was discovered, but I knew the instant the attention signal sounded that the situation was serious. Kincaide, my second officer, had a cool head, and he would not have called me except in a tremendous emergency.

"Hanson speaking!" I snapped into the microphone. "What's up, Mr. Kincaide?"

"A field of meteorites sweeping into our path, sir." Kincaide's voice was tense. "I have altered our course as much as I dared and am reducing speed at emergency rate, but this is the largest swarm of meteorites I have ever seen. I am afraid that we must pass through at least a section of it."

"With you in a moment, Mr. Kincaide!" I dropped the microphone and snatched up my robe, knotting its cord about me as I hurried out of my stateroom. In those days, interplanetary ships did not have their auras of repulsion rays to protect them from meteorites, it must be remembered. Two skins of metal were all that lay between the *Ertak* and all the dangers of space.

I took the companionway to the navigating room two steps at a time and fairly burst into the room.

Kincaide was crouched over the two charts that pictured the space around us, microphone pressed to his lips. Through the plate glass partition I could see the men in the operating room tensed over their wheels and levers and dials. Kincaide glanced up as I entered, and motioned with his free hand towards the charts.

One glance convinced me that he had not overestimated our danger. The space to right and left, and above and below, was fairly peppered with tiny pricks of greenish light that moved slowly across the milky faces of the charts.

From the position of the ship, represented as a glowing red spark, and measuring the distances roughly by means of the fine black lines graved in both directions upon the surface of the chart, it was evident to any understanding observer that disaster of a most terrible kind was imminent.

Kincaide muttered into his microphone, and out of the tail of my eye I could see his orders obeyed on the instant by the men in the operating room. I could feel the peculiar, sickening surge that told of speed being reduced, and the course being altered, but the cold, brutally accurate charts before me assured me that no action we dared take would save us from the meteorites.

"We're in for it, Mr. Kincaide. Continue to reduce speed as much as possible, and keep bearing away, as at present. I believe we can avoid the thickest portion of the field, but we shall have to take our chances with the fringe."

"Yes, sir!" said Kincaide, without lifting his eyes from the chart. His voice was calm and businesslike, now; with the responsibility on my shoulders, as commander, he was the efficient, level-headed thinking machine that had endeared him to me as both fellow-officer and friend.

Leaving the charts to Kincaide, I sounded the general emergency signal, calling every man and officer of the *Ertak's* crew to his post, and began giving orders through the microphone.

"Mr. Correy,"—Correy was my first officer—"please report at once to the navigating room. Mr. Hendricks, make the rounds of all duty posts, please, and give special attention to the disintegrator ray operators. The ray generators are to be started at once, full speed." Hendricks, I might say, was a junior officer, and a very good one, although quick-tempered and excitable—failings of youth. He had only recently shipped with us to replace Anderson Croy, who—but that has already been recorded.[2]

[2] "The Dark Side of Antri," in the January, 1931, issue of Astounding Stories.

These preparations made, I glanced at the twin charts again. The peppering of tiny green lights, each of which represented a meteoritic body, had definitely shifted in relation to the position of the strongly-glowing red spark that was the *Ertak*, but a quick comparison of the two charts showed that we would be certain to pass through—again I use land terms to make my meaning clear—the upper right fringe of the field.

The great cluster of meteorites was moving in the same direction as ourselves now; Kincaide's change of course had settled that matter nicely. Naturally, this was the logical course, since should we come in contact with any of them, the impact would bear a relation to only the *difference* in our speeds, instead of the *sum*, as would be the case if we struck at a wide angle.

It was difficult to stand without grasping a support of some kind, and walking was almost impossible, for the reduction of our tremendous speed, and even the slightest change of direction, placed terrific strains upon the ship and everything in it. Space ships, at space speeds, must travel like the old-fashioned bullets if those within are to feel at ease.

"I believe, Mr. Kincaide, it might be well to slightly increase the power in the gravity pads," I suggested. Kincaide nodded and spoke briefly into his microphone; an instant later I felt my weight increase perhaps fifty per cent, and despite the inertia of my body, opposed to both the change in speed and direction of the *Ertak*, I could now stand without support, and could walk without too much difficulty.

The door of the navigating room was flung open, and Correy entered, his face alight with curiosity and eagerness. An emergency meant danger, and few beings in the universe have loved danger more than Correy.

"We're in for it, Mr. Correy," I said, with a nod towards the charts. "Swarm of meteorites, and we can't avoid them."

"Well, we've dodged through them before, sir," smiled Correy. "We can do it again."

"I hope so, but this is the largest field of them I have ever seen. Look at the charts: they're thicker than flies."

Correy glanced at the charts, slapped Kincaide across his bowed, tense shoulders, and laughed aloud.

"Trust the old *Ertak* to worm her way through, sir," he said. "The ray crews are on duty, I presume?"

"Yes. But I doubt that the rays will be of much assistance to us. Particularly if these are stony meteorites—and as you know, the odds are about ten to one against their being of ferrous composition. The rays, deducting the losses due to the utter lack of a conducting medium, will be insufficient protection. They will help, of course. The iron meteorites they will take care of effectively, but the conglomerate nature of the stony meteorites does not make them particularly susceptible to the disintegrating rays.

"We shall do what we can, but our success will depend largely upon good luck—or Divine Providence."

"At any rate, sir," replied Correy, and his voice had lost some of its lightness, "we are upon routine patrol and not upon special mission. If we do crack up, there is no emergency call that will remain unanswered."

"No," I said dryly. "There will be just another 'Lost in Space' report in the records of the Service, and the *Ertak's* name will go up on the tablet of lost ships. In any case, we have done and shall do what we can. In ten minutes we shall know all there is to know. That about right, Mr. Kincaide?"

"Ten minutes?" Kincaide studied the charts with narrowed eyes, mentally balancing distance and speed. "We should be within the danger area in about that length of time, sir," he answered. "And out of it—if we come out—three or four minutes later."

"We'll come out of it," said Correy positively.

I walked heavily across the room and studied the charts again. Space above and below, to the right and the left of us, was powdered with the green points of light.

Correy joined me, his feet thumping with the unaccustomed weight given him by the increase in gravity. As he bent over the charts, I heard him draw in his breath sharply.

Kincaide looked up. Correy looked up. I looked up. The glance of each man swept the faces, read the eyes, of the other two. Then, with one accord, we all three glanced up at the clocks—more properly, at the twelve-figured dial of the Earth clock, for none of us had any great love for the metric Universal system of time-keeping.

Ten minutes.... Less than that, now.

"Mr. Correy," I said, as calmly as I could, "you will relieve Mr. Kincaide as navigating officer. Mr. Kincaide, present my compliments to Mr. Hendricks, and ask him to explain the situation to the crew. You will instruct the disintegrator ray operators in their duties, and take charge of their activities. Start operation at your discretion; you understand the necessity."

"Yes, sir!" Kincaide saluted sharply, and I returned his salute. We did not shake hands, the Earth gesture of—strangely enough—both greeting and farewell, but we both realized that this might well be a final parting. The door closed behind him, and Correy and I were left together to watch the creeping hands of the Earth clock, the twin charts with their thick spatter of green lights, and the two fiery red sparks, one on each chart, that represented the *Ertak* sweeping recklessly towards the swarming danger ahead.

In other accounts of my experiences in the Special Patrol Service I feel that I have written too much about myself. After all, I have run my race; a retired commander of the Service, and an old, old man, with the century mark well behind me, my only use is to record, in this fashion, some of those things the

Service accomplished in the old days when the worlds of the Universe were strange to each other, and space travel was still an adventure to many.

The Universe is not interested in old men; it is concerned only with youth and action. It forgets that once we were young men, strong, impetuous, daring. It forgets what we did; but that has always been so. It always will be so. John Hanson, retired Commander of the Special Patrol Service, is fit only to amuse the present generation with his tales of bygone days.

Well, so be it. I am content. I have lived greatly; certainly I would not exchange my memories of those bold, daring days even for youth and strength again, had I to live that youth and waste that strength in this softened, gilded age.

But no more of this; it is too easy for an old man to rumble on about himself. It is only the young John Hanson, Commander of the *Ertak*, who can interest those who may pick up and read what I am writing here.

I did not waste the minutes measured by that clock, grouped with our other instruments in the navigating room of the *Ertak*. I wrote hastily in the ship's log, stating the facts briefly and without feeling. If we came through, the log would read better thus; if not, and by some strange chance it came to human eyes, then the Universe would know at least that the *Ertak's* officers did not flinch from even such a danger.

As I finished the entry, Correy spoke:

"Kincaide's estimate was not far off, sir," he said, with a swift glance at the clock. "Here we go!" It was less than half a minute short of the ten estimated by Kincaide.

I nodded and bent over the television disc—one of the huge, hooded affairs we used in those days. Widening the field to the greatest angle, and with low power, I inspected the space before us on all sides.

The charts, operated by super-radio reflexes, had not lied about the danger into which we were passing—had passed. We were in the midst of a veritable swarm of meteorites of all sizes.

They were not large; I believe the largest I saw had a mass of not more than three or four times that of the *Ertak* herself. Some of the smaller bodies were only fifty or sixty feet in diameter.

They were jagged and irregular in shape, and they seemed to spin at varying speeds, like tiny worlds.

As I watched, fixing my view now on the space directly in our path, I saw that our disintegrator ray men were at work. Deep in the bowels of the *Ertak*, the moan of the ray generators had deepened in note; I could even feel the slight vibration beneath my feet.

One of the meteorites slowly crumbled on top, the dust of disintegration hovering in a compact mass about the body. More and more of it melted away. The spinning motion grew irregular, eccentric, as the center of gravity was changed by the action of the ray.

Another ray, two more, centered on the wobbling mass. It was directly in our path, looming up larger and larger every second.

Faster and faster it melted, the rays eating into it from four sides. But it was perilously near now; I had to reduce power in order to keep all of it within the field of my disc. If—

The thing vanished before the very nose of the ship, not an instant too soon. I glanced up at the surface temperature indicator, and saw the big black hand move slowly for a degree or two, and stop. It was a very sensitive instrument, and registered even the slight friction of our passage through the disintegrated dust of the meteorite.

Our rays were working desperately, but disintegrator rays are not nearly so effective in space as in an atmosphere of some kind. Half a dozen times it seemed that we must crash head on into one of the flying bodies, but our speed was reduced now to such an extent that we were going but little faster than the meteorites, and this fact was all that saved us. We had more time for utilizing our rays.

We nosed upward through the trailing fringe of the swarm in safety. The great field of meteorites was now below and ahead of us. We had won through! The *Ertak* was safe, and—

"There seems to be another directly above us, sir," commented Correy quietly, speaking for the first time since we had entered the area of danger. "I believe your disc is not picking it up."

"Thank you, Mr. Correy," I said. While operating on an entirely different principle, his two charts had certain very definite advantages: they showed the entire space around us, instead of but a portion.

I picked up the meteorite he had mentioned without difficulty. It was a large body, about three times the mass of the *Ertak*, and some distance above us— a laggard in the group we had just eluded.

"Will it coincide with our path at any point, Mr. Correy?" I asked doubtfully. The television disc could not, of course, give me this information.

"I believe so; yes," replied Correy, frowning over his charts. "Are the rays on it, sir?"

"Yes. All of them, I judge, but they are making slow work of it." I fell silent, bending lower over the great hooded disc.

There were a dozen, a score of rays playing upon the surface of the meteorite. A halo of dust hung around the rapidly diminishing body, but still the mass melted all too slowly.

Pressing the attention signal for Kincaide, I spoke sharply into the microphone:

"Mr. Kincaide, is every ray on that large meteorite above us?"

"Yes, sir," he replied instantly.

"Full power?"

"Yes, sir."

"Very well; carry on, Mr. Kincaide." I turned to Correy; he had just glanced from his charts to the clock, with its jerking second hand, and back to his charts.

"They'll have to do it in the next ten seconds, sir," he said. "Otherwise—" Correy shrugged, and his eyes fixed with a peculiar, fascinated stare on the charts. He was looking death squarely in the eyes.

Ten seconds! It was not enough. I had watched the rays working, and I knew their power to disintegrate this death-dealing stone that was hurtling along above us while we rose, helplessly, into its path.

I did not ask Correy if it was possible to alter the course enough, and quickly enough, to avoid that fateful path. Had it been possible without tearing the *Ertak* to pieces with the strain of it, Correy would have done it seconds ago.

I glanced up swiftly at the relentless, jerking second hand. Seven seconds gone! Three seconds more.

The rays were doing all that could be expected of them. There was only a tiny fragment of the meteorite left, and it was dwindling swiftly. But our time was passing even more rapidly.

The bit of rock loomed up at me from the disc. It seemed to fly up into my face, to meet me.

"Got us, Correy!" I said hoarsely. "Good-by, old-man!"

I think he tried to reply. I saw his lips open; the flash of the bright light from the ethon tubes on his big white teeth.

Then there was a crash that shook the whole ship. I shot into the air. I remember falling ... terribly.

A blinding flash of light that emanated from the very center of my brain, a sickening sense of utter catastrophe, and ... blackness.

I think I was conscious several seconds before I finally opened my eyes. My mind was still wandering; my thoughts kept flying around in huge circles that kept closing in.

We had hit the meteorite. I remembered the crash. I remembered falling. I remembered striking my head.

But I was still alive. There was air to breathe and there was firm material under me. I opened my eyes.

For the first instant, it seemed I was in an utterly strange room. Nothing was familiar. Everything was—was *inverted*. Then I glanced upward, and I saw what had happened.

I was lying on the ceiling of the navigating room. Over my head were the charts, still glowing, the chronometers in their gimballed beds, and the television disc. Beside me, sprawled out limply, was Correy, a trickle of dried blood on his cheek. A litter of papers, chairs, framed licenses and other movable objects were strewn on and around us.

My first instinctive, foolish thought was that the ship was upside down. Man has a ground-trained mind, no matter how many years he may travel space. Then, of course, I realized that in the open void there is not top nor bottom; the illusion is supplied, in space ships, by the gravity pads. Somehow, the shock of impact had reversed the polarity of the leads to the pads, and they had become repulsion pads. That was why I had dropped from the floor to the ceiling.

All this flashed through my mind in an instant as I dragged myself toward Correy. Dragged myself because my head was throbbing so that I dared not stand up, and one shoulder, my left, was numb.

For an instant I thought that Correy was dead. Then, as I bent over him, I saw a pulse leaping just under the angle of his jaw.

"Correy, old man!" I whispered. "Do you hear me?" All the formality of the Service was forgotten for the time. "Are you hurt badly?"

His eyelids flickered, and he sighed; then, suddenly, he looked up at me—and smiled!

"We're still here, sir?"

"After a fashion. Look around; see what's happened?"

He glanced about curiously, frowning. His wits were not all with him yet.

"We're in a mess, aren't we?" he grinned. "What's the matter?"

I told him what I thought, and he nodded slowly, feeling his head tenderly.

"How long ago did it happen?" he asked. "The blooming clock's upside down; can you read it?"

I could—with an effort.

"Over twenty minutes," I said. "I wonder how the rest of the men are?"

With an effort, I got to my feet and peered into the operating room. Several of the men were moving about, dazedly, and as I signalled to them, reassuringly, a voice hailed us from the doorway:

"Any orders, sir?"

It was Kincaide. He was peering over what had been the top of the doorway, and he was probably the most disreputable-looking officer who had ever worn the blue-and-silver uniform of the Service. His nose was bloody and swollen to twice its normal size. Both eyes were blackened, and his hair, matted with blood, was plastered in ragged swirls across his forehead.

"Yes, Mr. Kincaide; plenty of them. Round up enough of the men to locate the trouble with the gravity pads; there's a reversed connection somewhere. But don't let them make the repairs until the signal is given. Otherwise, we'll all fall on our heads again. Mr. Correy and I will take care of the injured."

The next half hour was a trying one. Two men had been killed outright, and another died before we could do anything to save him. Every man in the crew was shaken up and bruised, but by the time the check was completed, we had a good half of our personnel on duty.

Returning at last to the navigating room, I pressed the attention signal for Kincaide, and got his answer immediately.

"Located the trouble yet, Mr. Kincaide?" I asked anxiously.

"Yes, sir! Mr. Hendricks has been working with a group of men and has just made his report. They are ready when you are."

"Good!" I drew a sigh of relief. It had been easier than I thought. Pressing the general attention signal, I broadcasted the warning, giving particular instructions to the men in charge of the injured. Then I issued orders to Hendricks:

"Reverse the current in five seconds, Mr. Hendricks, and stand by for further instructions."

Hastily, then, Correy and I followed the orders we had given the men. Briefly we stood on our heads against the wall, feeling very foolish, and dreading the fall we knew was coming.

It came. We slid down the wall and lit heavily on our feet, while the litter that had been on the ceiling with us fell all around us. Miraculously, the ship seemed to have righted herself. Correy and I picked ourselves up and looked around.

"We're still operating smoothly," I commented with a sweeping glance at the instruments over the operating table. "Everything seems in order."

"Did you notice the speed indicator, sir?" asked Correy grimly. "When he fell, one of the men in the operating room must have pulled the speed lever all the way over. We're at maximum space speed, sir, and have been for nearly an hour, with no one at the controls."

We stared at each other dully. Nearly an hour, at maximum space speed—a speed seldom used except in case of great emergency. With no one at the controls, and the ship set at maximum deflection from her course.

That meant that for nearly an hour we had been sweeping into infinite space in a great arc, at a speed I disliked to think about.

"I'll work out our position at once," I said, "and in the meantime, reduce speed to normal as quickly as possible. We must get back on our course at the earliest possible moment."

We hurried across to the charts that were our most important aides in proper navigation. By comparing the groups of stars there with our space charts of the universe, the working out of our position was ordinarily, a simple matter.

But now, instead of milky rectangles, ruled with fine black lines, with a fiery red speck in the center and the bodies of the universe grouped around in green points of light, there were only nearly blank rectangles, shot through with vague, flickering lights that revealed nothing except the presence of disaster.

"The meteoric fragment wiped out some of our plates, I imagine," said Correy slowly. "The thing's useless."

I nodded, staring down at the crawling lights on the charts.

"We'll have to set down for repairs, Mr. Correy. If," I added, "we can find a place."

Correy glanced up at the attraction meter.

"I'll take a look in the big disc," he suggested. "There's a sizeable body off to port. Perhaps our luck's changed."

He bent his head under the big hood, adjusting the controls until he located the source of the registered attraction.

"Right!" he said, after a moment's careful scrutiny. "She's as big as Earth, I'd venture, and I believe I can detect clouds, so there should be atmosphere. Shall we try it, sir?"

"Yes. We're helpless until we make repairs. As big as Earth, you said? Is she familiar?"

Correy studied the image under the hood again, long and carefully.

"No, sir," he said, looking up and shaking his head. "She's a new one on me."

Conning the ship first by means of the television disc, and navigating visually as we neared the strange sphere, we were soon close enough to make out the physical characteristics of this unknown world.

Our spectroscopic tests had revealed the presence of atmosphere suitable for breathing, although strongly laden with mineral fumes which, while possibly objectionable, would probably not be dangerous.

So far as we could see, there was but one continent, somewhat north of the equator, roughly triangular in shape, with its northernmost point reaching nearly to the Pole.

"It's an unexplored world, sir. I'm certain of that," said Correy. "I am sure I would have remembered that single, triangular continent had I seen it on any of our charts." In those days, of course, the Universe was by no means so well mapped as it is today.

"If not unknown, it is at least uncharted," I replied. "Rough looking country, isn't it? No sign of life, either, that the disc will reveal."

"That's as well, sir. Better no people than wild natives who might interfere with our work. Any choice in the matter of a spot on which to set her down?"

I inspected the great, triangular continent carefully. Towards the north it was a mass of snow covered mountains, some of them, from their craters, dead volcanoes. Long spurs of these ranges reached southward, with green and apparently fertile valleys between. The southern edge was covered with dense tropical vegetation; a veritable jungle.

"At the base of that central spur there seems to be a sort of plateau," I suggested. "I believe that would be a likely spot."

"Very well, sir," replied Correy, and the old *Ertak*, reduced to atmospheric speed, swiftly swept toward the indicated position, while Correy kept a wary eye on the surface temperature gauge, and I swept the terrain for any sign of intelligent life.

I found a number of trails, particularly around the base of the foothills, but they were evidently game trails, for there were no dwelling places of any kind; no cities, no villages, not even a single habitation of any kind that the searching eyes of the disc could detect.

Correy set her down as neatly and as softly as a rose petal drifts to the ground. Roses, I may add, are a beautiful and delicate flower, with very soft petals, peculiar to my native Earth.

We opened the main exit immediately. I watched the huge, circular door back slowly out of its threads, and finally swing aside, swiftly and silently, in the grip of its mighty gimbals, with the weird, unearthly feeling I have always had when about to step foot on some strange star where no man has trod before.

The air was sweet, and delightfully fresh after being cooped up for weeks in the *Ertak*, with her machine-made air. A little thinner, I should judge, than the air to which we were accustomed, but strangely exhilarating, and laden with a faint scent of some unknown constituent—undoubtedly the mineral element our spectroscope had revealed but not identified. Gravity, I found upon passing through the exit, was normal. Altogether an extremely satisfactory repair station.

Correy's guess as to what had happened proved absolutely accurate. Along the top of the *Ertak*, from amidships to within a few feet of her pointed stem, was a jagged groove that had destroyed hundreds of the bright, coppery discs, set into the outer skin of the ship, that operated our super-radio reflex charts. The groove was so deep, in places, that it must have bent the outer skin of the *Ertak* down against the inner skin. A foot or more—it was best not to think of what would have happened then.

By the time we completed our inspection dusk was upon us—a long, lingering dusk, due, no doubt, to the afterglow resulting from the mineral content of the air. I'm no white-skinned, stoop-shouldered laboratory man, so I'm not sure that was the real reason. It sounds logical, however.

"Mr. Correy, I think we shall break out our field equipment and give all men not on watch an opportunity to sleep out in the fresh air," I said. "Will you give the orders, please?"

"Yes, sir. Mr. Hendricks will stand the eight to twelve watch as usual?"

I nodded.

"Mr. Kincaide will relieve him at midnight, and you will take over at four."

"Very well, sir." Correy turned to give the orders, and in a few minutes an orderly array of shelter tents made a single street in front of the fat, dully-gleaming side of the *Ertak*. Our tents were at the head of this short company street, three of them in a little row.

After the evening meal, cooked over open fires, with the smoke of the very resinous wood we had collected hanging comfortably in the still air, the men gave themselves up to boisterous, noisy games, which, I confess, I should have liked very much to participate in. They raced and tumbled around the two big fires like schoolboys on a lark. Only those who have spent most of their days in the metal belly of a space ship know the sheer joy of utter physical freedom.

Correy, Kincaide and I sat before our tents and watched them, chatting about this and that—I have long since forgotten what. But I shall never forget what occurred just before the watch changed that night. Nor will any man of the *Ertak's* crew.

It was just a few minutes before midnight. The men had quieted down and were preparing to turn in. I had given orders that this first night they could suit themselves about retiring; a good officer, and I tried to be one, is never afraid to give good men a little rein, now and then.

The fires had died down to great heaps of red coals, filmed with ashes, and, aside from the brilliant galaxy of stars overhead, there was no light from above. Either this world had no moons, not even a single moon, like my native Earth, or it had not yet arisen.

Kincaide rose lazily, stretched himself, and glanced at his watch.

"Seven till twelve, sir," he said. "I believe I'll run along and relieve—"

He never finished that sentence. From somewhere there came a rushing sound, and a damp, stringy net, a living, horrible, *something*, descended upon us out of the night.

In an instant, what had been an orderly encampment became a bedlam. I tried to fight against the stringy, animated, nearly intangible mass, or masses, that held me, but my arms, my legs, my whole body, was bound as with strings and loops of elastic bands.

Strange whispering sounds filled the air, audible above the shouting of the men. The net about me grew tighter; I felt myself being lifted from the ground. Others were being treated the same way; one of the *Ertak's* crew shot straight up, not a dozen feet away, writhing and squirming. Then, at an elevation of perhaps twice my height, he was hurried away.

Hendrick's voice called out my name from the *Ertak's* exit, and I shouted a warning:

"Hendrick! Go back! Close the emergency—" Then a gluey mass cut across my mouth, and, as though carried on huge soft springs, I was hurried away, with the sibilant, whispering sounds louder and closer than ever. With me, as nearly as I could judge, went every man who had not been on duty in the ship.

I ceased struggling, and immediately the rubbery network about me loosened. It seemed to me that the whisperings about me were suddenly approving. We were in the grip, then, of some sort of intelligent beings, ghost-like and invisible though they were.

After a time, during which we were all, in a ragged group, being borne swiftly towards the mountains, all at a common level from the ground, I managed to turn my head so that I could see, against the star-lit sky, something of the nature of the things that had made us captive.

As is not infrequently the case, in trying to describe things of an utterly different world, I find myself at a loss for words. I think of jellyfish, such as inhabit the seas of most of the inhabited planets, and yet this is not a good description.

These creatures were pale, and almost completely transparent. What their forms might be, I could not even guess. I could make out writhing, tentacle-like arms, and wrinkled, flabby excrudescences and that was all. That these creatures were huge, was evident from the fact that they, apparently walking, from the irregular, undulating motion, held us easily ten or a dozen feet from the ground.

With the release of the pressure about my body I was able to talk again, and I called out to Correy, who was fighting his way along, muttering, angrily, just ahead of me.

"Correy! No use fighting them. Save your strength, man!"

"Then? What are they, in God's name? What spawn of hell—"

"The Commander is right, Correy," interrupted Kincaide, who was not far from my first officer. "Let's get our breaths and try to figure out what's happened. I'm winded!" His voice gave plentiful evidence of the struggle he had put up.

"I want to know where I'm going, and why!" growled Correy, ceasing his struggling, nevertheless. "What have us? Are they fish or flesh or fowl?"

"I think we shall know before very long, Correy," I replied. "Look ahead!"

The bearers of the men in the fore part of the group had apparently stopped before a shadowy wall, like the face of a cliff. Rapidly, the rest of us were brought up, until we were in a compact group, some in sitting positions, some upside down, the majority reclining on back or side. The whispering sound now was intense and excited, as though our strange bearers awaited some momentous happening.

I took advantage of the opportunity to speak very briefly to my companions.

"Men, I'll admit frankly that I don't know what we're up against," I said. "But I do know this: we'll come out on top of the heap. Conserve your strength, keep your eyes open, and be prepared to obey, instantly, any orders that may be issued: I know that last remark is not needed. If any of you should see or learn something of interest or value, report at once to Mr. Correy, Mr. Kincaide or my—"

A simultaneous, involuntary exclamation from the men interrupted me, and it was not surprising that this was so, for the wall before us had suddenly opened, and there was a great burst of yellow light in our faces. A strong odor, like the faint scent we had first noticed in the air, but infinitely more powerful, struck our nostrils, but I was not conscious of the fact for several seconds. My whole attention, my every startled thought, was focused upon the group of strange beings, silhouetted against the glowing light, that stood in the opening.

Imagine, if you can, a huge globe, perhaps eight feet in diameter, flattened slightly at the bottom, and supported on six short, huge stumps, like the feet of an elephant, and topped by an excrudescence like a rounded coning tower, merging into the globular body. From points slightly below this excrudescence, visualize six long, limp tentacles, so long that they drop from the equators of these animated spheres, and trail on the ground. Now you have some conception of the beings that stood before us.

A sharp, sibilant whispering came from one of these figures, to be answered in an eager chorus from our bearers. There was a reply like a command, and the group in the doorway marched forward. One by one these visible tentacles wrapped themselves around a member of the *Ertak's* crew, each one of the globular creatures bearing one of us.

I heard a disappointed whisper go up from the outer darkness where, but a moment before, we had been. Then there was a grating sound, and a thud as the stone doorway was rolled back into place.

The entrance was sealed. We were prisoners indeed!

"All right, now what?" gritted Correy. "God! If I ever get a hand loose!"

Swiftly, each of us held above the head-like excrudescence atop the globular body of the thing that held us, we were carried down a widening rocky corridor, towards the source of the yellow light that beat about us.

The passage led to a great cavern, irregular in shape, and apparently possessed of numerous other outlets which converged here.

I am not certain as to the size of the cavern, save that it was great, and that the roof was so high in most sections that it was lost in shadow.

The great cavern was nearly filled with creatures similar to those which were bearing us, and they fell back in orderly passage to permit our conductors to pass.

I could see, now, that the hump atop each rounded body was a travesty of a head, hairless, and without a neck. Their features were particularly hideous, and I shall pass over a description as rapidly as possible.

The eyes were round, and apparently lidless; a pale drab or bluff in color. Instead of a nose, as, we understand the term, they had a convoluted rosette in the center of the face, not unlike the olfactory organ of a bat. Their ears were placed as are ours, but were of thin, pale parchment, and hugged the side of the head tightly. Instead of a mouth, there was a slightly depressed oval of fluttering skin near the point where the head melted into the rounded body: the rapid fluttering or vibration of this skin produced the whispering sound I have already remarked.

The cavern, as I have said, was flooded with yellow light, which came from a great column of fire near the center of the clear space. I had no opportunity to inspect the exact arrangements but from what I did see, I judged that this flame was fed by some sort of highly inflammable substance, not unlike crude oil, except that it burned clearly and without smoke. This substance was conducted to the font from which the flame leaped by means of a large pipe of hollow reed or wood.

At the far end of the cavern a procession entered from one of the passages— nine figures similar to those which bore us, save that by the greater darkness of their skin, and the wrinkles upon both face and body, I judged these to be older than the rest. From the respect with which they were treated, and the dignity of their movements, I gathered that these were persons of authority, a surmise which quickly verified itself.

These nine elders arranged themselves, standing, in the form of a semicircle, the center creature standing a pace or two in front of the others. At a whispered command, we were all dumped unceremoniously on the floor of the cavern before this august council of nine.

Nine pairs of fish-like, unblinking eyes inspected us, whether with enmity or otherwise; I could not determine. One of the nine spoke briefly to one of our conductors, and received an even more brief reply.

I felt the gaze of the creature in the center fix on me. I had taken my proper position in front of my men; he apparently recognized me as the leader of the group.

In a sharp whisper, he addressed me; I gathered from the tone that he uttered a command, but I could only shake my head in response. No words could convey thought from his mind to mine—but we did have a means of communication at hand.

"Mr. Correy," I said, "your menore, please!" I released my own from the belt which held it, along with the other expeditionary equipment which we always wore when outside our ship, and placed it in position upon my head, motioning for one of the nine to do likewise with Correy's menore.

They watched me suspiciously, despite my attempt to convey, by gestures, that by means of these instruments we could convey thoughts to each other. The menores of those days were bulky, heavy things, and undoubtedly they looked dangerous to these creatures: thought-transference instruments at that time were complicated affairs.

However, I must have made myself partially understood, at least, for the chief of the nine uttered a whispered command to one of the beings who had borne us to the large cavern, and motioned with a writhing gesture of one tentacle that I was to place the menore upon this creature's head.

"The old boy's playing it safe, sir," muttered Correy, chuckling. "Wants to try it out on the dog first."

"Right!" I nodded, and, not without difficulty, placed the other menore upon the rounded dome of the individual selected for the trial.

Both instruments were adjusted to full power, and I concentrated my mental energy upon the simple pictures that I thought I could convey to the limited mentality of which I suspected these creatures, watching his fishy eyes the while.

It was several seconds before he realized what was happening; then he began talking excitedly to the waiting nine. The words fairly burned themselves in my consciousness, but of course were utterly unintelligible to me. Before the creature had finished, a lash-like tentacle shot out from the chief of the nine and removed the menore; a moment later it reposed, at a rather rakish slant, on the shining dome of its new possessor.

"Get anything, sir?" asked Correy in a low voice.

"Not yet. I'm trying to make him see how we came here, and that we're friends. Then I'll see what I can get out of him; he'll have to get the idea of coming back at me with pictures instead of words, and it may take a long time to make him understand."

It did take a long time. I could feel the sweat trickling down my face as I strove to make him understand. His eyes revealed wonderment and a little fear, but an almost utter lack of understanding.

I pictured for him the heavens, and our ship sailing along through space. Then I showed him the *Ertak* coming to rest on the plateau, and he made little impatient noises as though to convey that he knew all about that.

After a long time he got the idea. Crudely, dimly, he pictured the *Ertak* leaving this strange world, and soaring off into vacant space. Then his scene faded out, and he pictured the same thing again, as one might repeat a question not understood. He wanted to know where we would go if we left this world of his.

I pictured for him other worlds, peopled with men more or less like myself. I showed him the great cities, and the fleets of ships like the *Ertak* that plied between them. Then, as best I could, I asked him about himself and his people.

It came to me jerkily and poorly pictured, but I managed to piece out the story. Whether I guess correctly on all points, I am not sure, nor will I ever be sure. But this is the story as I got it.

These people at one time lived in the open, and all the people of this world were like those in the cavern, possessed of opaque bodies and great strength. There were none of the ghost-like creatures who had captured us.

But after a long time, a ruling class arose. They tried to dominate the masses, and the masses refused to be dominated. But the ruling classes were wise, and versed in certain sciences; the masses were ignorant. So the ruling classes devised a plan.

These creatures did not eat. There was a tradition that at one time they had had mouths, as I had, but that was not known. Their strength, their vitality, came from the powerful mineral vapor which came forth from the bowels of the earth. The ruling classes decided that if they could control the supply of this vapor, they would have the whip hand, and they set about realizing this condition.

It was quickly done. All the sources of supply, save one, were sealed. This one source of supply was the cavern in which we stood. These were members of the ruling class, and outside was the rabble, starved and unhappy, living on the faint seepage of the vital fumes, without which they became almost bodiless, and the helpless slaves of those within the cavern.

These creatures, then, were boneless; as boneless as sponges, and, like sponges, capable of absorbing huge quantities of a foreign substance, which distended them and gave them weight. I could see, now, why the rotund bodies sagged and flattened at the base, and why six short, stubby legs were needed to support that body. There was only tissue, unsupported by bone, to bear the weight!

This chief of the nine went on to show me how ruthlessly, how cruelly those within the cavern ruled those without. The substance that fed the flame had to be gathered and a great reservoir on the side of the mountain kept filled. Great masses of dry, sweet grass, often changed, must be harvested and brought to the entrance of the cavern, for bedding. A score of other tasks kept the outsiders busy always—and the driving force was that, did the slaves become disobedient, the slight supply of mineral vapor available in the outside world would be cut off utterly, and all outside would surely die, slowly and in agony.

Those within the cavern were the rulers. They would always remain the rulers, and those outside would remain the slaves to wait upon them. And we—how strangely he pictured us, as he saw us!—were not to return to our queer worlds, that we might bring many other ships like the *Ertak* back to interfere. No.

The pupils of his eyes contracted, and the leafy structure of his nose fluttered as though with strong emotion.

No, we would not go back. He would give a signal to those of his creatures who stood behind us—a sort of soldiery, I gathered—and our heads, our legs, our arms, would be torn from our bodies. Then we would not go back to bring—

That was enough for me.

"Men!" I spoke softly, but with an intensity that gave me their instant attention, "it's going to be a fight for life. When I give the signal, make a rush for the entrance by which we came in. I'll lead the way. Use your pistols, and your bombs if necessary. All right—forward!"

Correy's great shout rang out after mine, and I flung my menore in the face of the nearest guard. It bounced off as though it had struck a rubber ball. Behind me, one of the men called out sharply; I heard a sharp crunch of bone, and with a pang realized that the *Ertak's* log would have at least one death to record.

A dozen tentacles lashed out at me, and I sprayed their owners with pellets from my atomic pistol. The air was filled with the shouts of my men and the whispers of our enemies. All around me I could hear the screaming of ricochets from our pistols. Twice atomic bombs exploded not far away, and the solid rock shook beneath my feet. Something shot by close to my face; an instant later a limp bundle in the blue and silver uniform of our Service struck the rock wall of the cavern, thirty feet away. The strength in those rubbery tentacles was terrible.

The pistols seemed to have but little effect. They wounded, but they did not kill unless the pellet struck the head. Then the victim rolled over, rocking idiotically on its middle.

"In the head, men!" I shouted. "That downs them! And keep the bombs in action. Throw them against the walls of the cavern. Take a chance!"

A ragged cheer went up, and I heard Correy's voice raised in angry conversation with the enemy:

"You will, eh? There!... Now!... Ah!—right—through—the—eye. That's—the place!"

A score of times I was grasped and held by the writhing arms of the angry horde whispering all around me. Each time I literally shot the tentacle away with my atomic pistol, leaving the severed end to unwrap itself and drop from my struggling body. The things had no blood in them.

Steadily, we fought our way toward the doorway, out of the cavern, down the passageway, pressed into a compact, sweating mass by the pressure of the eager bodies around us. I have never heard any sound even remotely like the babel of angry, sibilant whispering that beat against the walls and roof of that cavern.

I had saved my own bombs for a specific purpose, and now I unslung them and managed to work them up above my shoulders, one in either hand.

"I'm going to try to blow the entrance clear, men," I shouted. "The instant I fling the bombs, drop! The fragments will be stopped by the enemy crowding around us. One ... two ... three ... *drop*!"

The two bombs exploded almost simultaneously. The ground shook, and all over the cavern masses of stone came crashing to the floor. Bits of rock hummed and shrieked over our heads. And—yes! There was a draft of cooler, purer air on our faces. The bombs had done their work.

"One more effort and we're outside, men," I called. "The passage is open, and there are only a few of the enemy before us. Ready?"

"Ready!" went up the hoarse shout.

"Then, forward!"

It was easy to give the command, but hard to execute it. We were pressed so hard that only the men on the outside of the group could use their weapons. And our captors were making a terrible, desperate effort to hold us.

Two more of our men were literally torn to pieces before my eyes, but I had the satisfaction of ripping holes in the heads of the creatures whose tentacles had done the beastly work. And in the meantime we were working our way slowly but surely to the entrance.

I glanced up as I dodged out into the open. That soft humming sound was familiar, and properly so. There, at an elevation of less than fifty feet, was the *Ertak*, with Hendricks standing in the exit, leaning forward at a perilous angle.

"Ahoy the *Ertak*!" I hailed. "Descend at once!"

"Right, sir!" Hendricks turned to relay the order, and, as the rest of the men burst forth from the cavern, the ship struck the ground before us.

"All hands board ship!" I ordered. "Lively, now." As many years as I have commanded men, I have never seen an order obeyed with more alacrity.

I was the last man to enter, and as I did so, I turned for a last glance at the enemy.

They could not come through the small opening my bombs had driven in the rock, although they were working desperately to enlarge it. Leaping back and forth between me and the entrance I could see the vague, shadowy figures of the outside slaves, eagerly seeping up the life-giving fumes that escaped from the cavern.

"Your orders, sir?" asked Hendricks anxiously; he was a very young officer, and he had been through a very trying experience.

"Ascend five hundred feet, Mr. Hendricks," I said thoughtfully. "Directly over this spot. Then I'll take over.

"It isn't often," I added, "that the Service concerns itself with economic conditions. This, however, is one of the exceptions."

"Yes, sir," said Hendricks, for the very good reason, I suppose, that that was about all a third officer could say to his commander, under the circumstances.

"Five hundred feet, sir," said Hendricks.

"Very well," I nodded, and pressed the attention signal of the non-commissioned officer in charge of the big forward ray projector.

"Ott? Commander Hanson speaking. I have special orders for you."

"Yes, sir!"

"Direct your ray, narrowed to normal beam and at full intensity, on the spot directly below. Keep the ray motionless, and carry on until further orders. Is that clear?"

"Perfectly, sir." The disintegrator ray generators deepened their purr as I turned away.

"I trust, sir, that I did the right thing in following you with the *Ertak*?" asked Hendricks. "I was absolutely without precedent, and the circumstances were so mysterious—"

"You handled the situation very well indeed," I told him. "Had you not been waiting when we fought our way into the open, the nearly invisible things on the outside might have—but you don't know about them yet."

Picking up the microphone again, I ordered a pair of searchlights to follow the disintegrator ray, and made my way forward, where I could observe activities through a port.

The ray was boring straight down into a shoulder of a rocky hill, and the bright beams of the searchlights glowed redly with the dust of disintegration. Here and there I could see the shadowy, transparent forms of the creatures that the self-constituted rulers of this world had doomed to a demi-existence, and I smiled grimly to myself. The tables would soon be turned.

For perhaps an hour the ray melted its way into the solid rock, while I stood beside Ott and his crew, watching. Then, down below us, things began to happen.

Little fragments of rock flew up from the shaft the ray had drilled. Jets of black mud leaped into the air. There was a sudden blast from below that rocked the *Ertak*, and the shaft became a miniature volcano, throwing rocky fragments and mud high into the air.

"Very good, Ott," I said triumphantly. "Cease action." As I spoke, the first light of the dawn, unnoticed until now, spread itself over the scene, and we witnessed then one of the strangest scenes that the Universe has ever beheld.

Up to the very edge of that life-giving blast of mineral-laden gas the tenuous creatures came crowding. There were hundreds of them, thousands of them. And they were still coming, crowding closer and closer and closer, a mass of crawling, yellowish shadows against the sombre earth.

Slowly, they began to fill out and darken, as they drew in the fumes that were more than bread and meat and water to us. Where there had been formless shadows, rotund creatures such as we had met in the cavern stood and lashed their tentacles about in a sort of frenzied gladness, and fell back to make room for their brothers.

"It's a sight to make a man doubt his own eyes, sir," said Correy, who had come to stand beside me. "Look at them! Thousands of them pouring from every direction. How did it happen?"

"It didn't happen. I used our disintegrator ray as a drill; we simply sunk a huge shaft down into the bowels of the earth until we struck the source of the vapor which the self-appointed 'ruling class' has bottled up. We have emancipated a whole people, Mr. Correy."

"I hate to think of what will happen to those in the cavern," replied Correy, smiling grimly. "Or rather, since you've told me of the pleasant little death they had arranged for us. I'm mighty glad of it. They'll receive rough treatment, I'm afraid!"

"They deserve it. It has been a great sight to watch, but I believe we've seen enough. It has been a good night's work, but it's daylight, now, and it will take hours to repair the damage to the *Ertak's* hull. Take over in the navigating room, if you will, and pick a likely spot where we will not be disturbed. We should be on our course by to-night, Mr. Correy."

"Right, sir," said Correy, with a last wondering look at the strange miracle we had brought to pass on the earth below us. "It will seem good to be off in space again, away from the troubles of these little worlds."

"There are troubles in space, too," I said dryly, thinking of the swarm of meteorites that had come so close to wiping the *Ertak* off the records of the Service. "You can't escape trouble even in space."

"No, sir," said Correy from the doorway. "But you can get your sleep regularly!"

And sleep is, when one comes to think of it, a very precious thing.

Particularly for an old man, whose eyelids are heavy with years.